TWENTIETH CENTURY
INTERPRETATIONS
OF

THE ICEMAN COMETH

TWENTIETH CENTURY INTERPRETATIONS
OF
THE ICEMAN COMETH

A Collection of Critical Essays

Edited by
JOHN HENRY RALEIGH

Prentice-Hall, Inc. *Englewood Cliffs, N. J.*
A SPECTRUM BOOK

Contents

PART TWO—*Interpretations*

TWENTIETH CENTURY
INTERPRETATIONS
OF
THE ICEMAN COMETH

Introduction

by John Henry Raleigh

1. The Life of Eugene O'Neill

Eugene O'Neill was born on October 16, 1888 on the third floor of Barrett House, a hotel on Times Square in New York City. His father, James O'Neill, was a well-known and successful actor, most famous for his role of Edmund Dantes in *The Count of Monte Cristo*. From 1888 to 1895, Eugene O'Neill traveled, under the care of a Scotch nurse, with his parents on theatrical road tours in cities all over the United States. From 1896 to 1900 he attended a Catholic private school, Mount St. Vincent-on-Hudson; in 1900-1902 he was enrolled in the De La Salle Military Institute and from 1902 to 1906 at Betts Academy in Stamford, Connecticut. In the 1880's, James O'Neill had had a summer home built—it was in fact the O'Neill's only "home"— for himself and his family in New London, Connecticut, at that time a rather fashionable summer resort. It was here that the family spent its summers. More importantly, this house provided the physical setting for O'Neill's great autobiographical tragedy, *Long Day's Journey Into Night,* in which he revealed and analyzed the various tragedies of his family: his mother's periodic dope addiction; his father's sense of frustration at having been seduced from becoming a great Shakespearean actor (as he was once on his way to becoming) by the financial lure of the popular *Monte Cristo*; his older brother's (Jamie) destructive and self-destructive traits which were later to lead him to drink himself to death; and his own mysticism, rebelliousness, fascination with death, obsession with human suffering and guilt, and sense of tragedy. Almost from the start O'Neill had, as a friend later remarked,

> . . . six senses. Sight, smell, taste, touch, hearing, and tragedy. The last is by far the most highly developed.[1]

O'Neill's formal schooling, except for one year, 1914 to 1915, at Harvard in the famous play-writing class of Professor George Baker,

[1] Hamilton Basso, "Profiles: The Tragic Sense," *New Yorker* XXIV, Feb. 28, 1948, 34.

ended when he left Princeton in 1907 in the spring of his freshman year, his departure being lamented by neither his teachers nor the college authorities. Between 1907 and 1912 he did a variety of things: worked at odd jobs; went on a gold prospecting trip in Honduras; went to sea as a deck hand several times; traveled with and worked for his father's acting company; married, fathered a child and divorced his wife; and lived for a time in destitution and alcoholism at "Jimmy the Priest's," a waterfront dive in New York (and one of the places which inspired *The Iceman Cometh*) where in 1912 he attempted to commit suicide. Nineteen hundred and twelve, the fictional date of both *The Iceman* and *Long Day's Journey*, was the seminal year of his life. On the 24th of December, his health broken, he entered a TB sanitarium. In May, 1913, he was discharged, an arrested case, but in the interval he had decided to become a playwright.

In the spring of 1914 he composed *Bound East for Cardiff*, a one-act play. His first fame came when this play was produced by the Provincetown Players in the summer of 1916. He captured Broadway in 1920 with his first full-length play, *Beyond the Horizon*, for which he was awarded the Pulitzer Prize. From then on his fame and his finances were assured. There followed in the 1920's and early 1930's a string of successes. To mention only the most well known: *The Emperor Jones, The Hairy Ape, Anna Christie, All God's Chillun Got Wings, Desire Under the Elms, Strange Interlude*, and *Mourning Becomes Electra*. But he punctuated these successes with some rather bad plays, such as *Welded, The Fountain*, and *Marco Millions*, and by the 1930's it began to appear that his initial creative outburst had run its course and that the talent that had created *The Emperor Jones* and *Desire Under the Elms* was drying up. When in 1934 the Theatre Guild, the company with which O'Neill had come to be permanently associated, produced *Days Without End*, probably O'Neill's worst play (although there are other candidates for this dubious distinction), the serious student of American drama might well have felt that the greatest American playwright had reached the end of the road, even though he was to receive the Nobel Prize in 1936. It was true that he had also written, in the middle of his struggle to compose the recalcitrant *Days Without End, Ah, Wilderness!* a charming and successful comedy. But comic plays had never been his aim or concern, although he was a first-rate comic writer, and in his work as a whole, *Ah, Wilderness!* is a sport. *Days Without End* is concerned with the problems of religious belief in the modern world and ends with the protagonist prostrate before a Cross in a Catholic Church. So too it might be said that O'Neill was prostrate, but not before a Cross; rather he seemed to be begging the Muse of the dramatic imagination to revisit him and re-invest him with the primal creative powers. (This wish was later to be granted.) At this point, however, he went into retirement, and another O'Neill play was not to be produced for twelve years (*The Iceman Cometh* in 1946).

O'Neill's personal life was as tumultuous, colorful, and tragedy-ridden as are his plays. He was married three times. Of his three children, two sons and one daughter by his first two marriages, only Oona O'Neill, now Mrs. Charles Chaplin, escaped the ancestral curse that seemed to haunt the O'Neill family and to mark out its members for destruction, self-inflicted or otherwise. Eugene O'Neill Jr., once a promising classical scholar and professor at Yale, ended as a suicide; Shane O'Neill, still living, has led what can only be described as a sad life; Eugene O'Neill III, son of Shane, died as an infant of "accidental suffocation."

O'Neill's lasting marriage was to Carlotta Monterey, whom he married in 1929. From this marriage ensued his final and characteristic style of life: isolation in a series of often splendid or sumptuous homes (which never became permanent). From 1929-1931 O'Neill lived in the "Chateau de Plessis" in Sainte Antoine du Roches, France; from 1932 to 1936 in "Casa Genotta," i.e., the Castle of Gene and Carlotta, in Sea Island, Georgia; from 1937 to 1943 in "Tao House" near Danville in Contra Costa County, California. Inside these elegant walls two things were going on in addition to the dynamics of the passionate and often difficult marital relationship; O'Neill was turning slowly but surely into a physical wreck and at the same time he was tortuously composing his greatest plays.

He suffered from a rare disease of the nervous system which progressively robbed him of motor control. The initial symptom was a trembling of the hands, a particularly tragic affliction for a writer who was ineluctably wedded to writing in long hand. Thus the late plays were written under great physical stress and anguish—on some days he could not write at all—and at least by 1947 he had to give up writing altogether, except for a few successful and sporadic attempts. By his death in 1953 he was a mind encased in an almost helpless body.

His dramatic ambitions had been immense. After the failure of *Days Without End,* he had decided that he could no longer deal with the present but would have to turn back to the past, and he turned back in two ways: to his own past and to American history. His overriding ambition was a great cycle of plays, something between nine and eleven, under the general title of *A Tale of Possessors Self-Dispossessed* covering American history from 1775 to the 1930's and detailing the lives of the successive generations of an Irish-American family. He had, in some form or other, written a great deal of this cycle when it became apparent that his disease would prevent his ever finishing the project. Fearful that someone else would attempt to finish these plays after his death, he, aided by his wife, tore up the manuscripts bit by bit. Only *A Touch of the Poet* was allowed to survive. By accident, and against O'Neill's express wishes, *More Stately Mansions*, unfinished, also survived. He had also planned a cycle of one-act plays under the general title *By Way of Obit*; of these only *Hughie* survived.

Between 1937 and 1943, in order to give himself respite from the demands of *A Tale of Possessors*, he intermittently turned back to his own past and wrote *The Iceman Cometh, Long Day's Journey Into Night*, and *A Moon for the Misbegotten* (based on the last days of his talented but disastrous older brother). These plays, fabled by the daughters of memory, are his finest. *Long Day's Journey* and *A Moon* were written in sorrow. In the Preface to *Long Day's Journey*, he speaks of "this play of old sorrow, written in tears and blood" and of the courage that the love of his wife gave him which enabled him to "face my dead at last" and to write the play, "with deep pity and understanding and forgiveness for *all* the four haunted Tyrones [O'Neills]." But *The Iceman Cometh*, despite its somber themes, was written in joy, in the pure pleasure of recapturing a past that he had himself once known but that was not connected with his family. According to his own testimony, the play flowed from his pen. (See the interview with Schriftgriesser below.) For he had found at the last that art for him was a species of autobiography: the remembrance of things past.

*   *   *

O'Neill died at the age of sixty-five in a hotel room in Boston. His last articulate words, uttered with clenched fists, were: "Born in a hotel room—and Goddamn it—died in a hotel room."

2. *The Biographical Genesis and the Literary Genre*

In their mammoth biography *O'Neill* (N.Y. 1960), Barbara and Arthur Gelb have reconstructed the varied autobiographical genesis of *The Iceman Cometh*. When O'Neill returned by ship to New York from Buenos Aires in 1912, he had twenty-five dollars, his seaman's wages, in his pocket. With a couple of shipmates he headed for a waterfront rooming house and saloon on Fulton Street near West Street opposite the West Washington Market. The rent was $3.00 per month, the vermin were omnipresent, and the company "choice":

sailors, whores, stevedores, Wobblies, anarchists, and various other kinds of bottom dogs. This was Jimmy the Priest's, so called because the proprietor, who was really a callous, cynical man, had an ascetic and priestly appearance. At this emporium a nickel would buy a schooner of beer or a shot of bad whiskey. "Gorky's *Night's Lodging*," said O'Neill, "was an ice cream parlor in comparison." [2] But he also later said that these riffraff were the best friends he ever had. O'Neill's room was unheated, lit by a kerosene light, and opened out through its one window onto a rickety fire escape. There were two beds in the room, so he had a succession of roommates. O'Neill spent no money on food, since roomers at Jimmy the Priest's were entitled to one free plate of soup per day, but subsisted on whiskey and the free soup. His female companions were whores, one of whom, named Maude, professed to be in love with him.

Here he first met some of the characters or prototypes of *The Iceman Cometh*. There was a drunken ex-British Army officer, Major Adams, whose chief diversion was reliving the Boer War and who became Captain Lewis of the play. Jimmy Cameron of *The Iceman* was suggested by one of O'Neill's roommates. This man, a Scot, had been a successful newspaper reporter and had covered the Boer War. Some "appalling" tragedy happened to him and he became an alcoholic. According to O'Neill:

> But always my friend—at least always when he had several jolts of liquor—saw a turn in the road tomorrow. He was going to get himself together and get back to work. Well, he did get a job and got fired. Then he realized that this tomorrow never would come. He solved everything by jumping to his death from the bedroom at Jimmy's.

As with Parritt in the play, the suicide was off the fire escape. Soon after this O'Neill himself made his suicide attempt with Veronal tablets. There are various versions of this story, but it seems apparent that it was not a wholehearted and unequivocal effort, such as usually succeed. About his days at Jimmy the Priest's, O'Neill was later to say:

> I lived with them, got to know them. In some queer way they carried on. I learned at Jimmy-the-Priest's not to sit in judgment on people. [3]

The second location to inspire *The Iceman Cometh* was a ramshackle hotel in Greenwich Village called The Golden Swan, but known to its denizens as the Hell Hole. Here in 1915, O'Neill met more of the characters in *The Iceman Cometh*: Tom Wallace (Harry Hope), the proprietor, who had connections with Tammany Hall, had known Richard Crocker, the Tammany boss, and seldom went

[2] Gelb, *O'Neill*, p. 162.
[3] Gelb, *O'Neill*, p. 171.

outside his saloon; "Happy" (Hickey), a collector for a laundry chain who visited the Hell Hole every Friday and dispensed cheer and free drinks (one Friday he did not turn up, having absconded with the laundry's money); Terry Carlin (Larry Slade), ex-syndicalist-anarchist, Irishman, Nietzschean philosopher, professional drinker, facile and brilliant talker, and a man who had a tremendous impact on O'Neill. The Gelbs suggest that Willie Oban of the play is a self-portrait of O'Neill himself who at this time was an alcoholic, sodden, self-destructive, and full of self-pity. If Terry Carlin had not periodically forced him to eat, he might in fact have drunk himself to death at this time.

Later, on January 22, 1918, after O'Neill's first success as a playwright, at a drinking party in this bar a young man named Louis Holliday, an ex-alcoholic who had temporarily cured himself but had lapsed back into drinking after a disappointment in love, procured a lethal dose of heroin from Terry Carlin and committed suicide. He died before the eyes of the people there. That Holliday had made Carlin, in a sense, his "executioner," and that Carlin had accepted the role, suggests, of course, the Parritt-Slade relationship in the play.

Finally, the Garden Hotel, across the street from the old Madison Square Garden, a bar which James O'Neill, Jamie O'Neill, and Eugene O'Neill all patronized over a number of years, also provided at least one other character for *The Iceman*: Bill Clarke (Ed Mosher), an old circus man. There was also a café in the Village that was headquarters for O'Neill and other intellectuals and writers. Its proprietress was Louis Holliday's sister, Polly, who at this time was the mistress of a Hungarian anarchist named Hippolyte Havel, who became in the play Hugo Kalmar. (See the essay by Doris Alexander.)

Such then were the raw materials out of which O'Neill constructed his play. It hardly needs to be added that most of these characters were not transferred literally or photographically into *The Iceman Cometh* but were altered or transmuted by O'Neill's dramatic imagination.

The references to Gorky, however, underline the fact that *The Iceman Cometh* not only is autobiographical but also falls into a well-recognized literary genre, the drama of "the lower depths." The roots of the human imagination's interest in the conditions of life at the lowest extremities of society probably stretch back into the archaic world itself, wherein it was believed that madmen, lunatics, outcasts were somehow holy or blessed, or possessed a knowledge that normal people did not have. In a more advanced society like ancient Greece, this same belief surfaces in a play like *Oedipus at Colonus,* in which the old blind beggar and outcast, once a great king and the greatest sinner that the mind can conjure up (slayer of his father, husband to his mother), has become, by dint of his sufferings, a holy person. His death is a transfiguration and the place wherein he is transfigured becomes a sacred spot. In more modern times it was the Romantic era, in the late eighteenth and early nineteenth centuries, that enshrined the murderer, the whore, the thief, the beggar, and the outcast as possessors of a kind of outlook or knowledge—what life is like in the depths—denied to commonplace normality. The prostitute with the heart of gold, the great sinner who is first-cousin to the great saint (both of these types are given their greatest expression in Dostoevsky, who had a profound influence on the youthful O'Neill), the idea that normal existence, especially middle-class existence, is one vast hypocritical sham which sweeps under the rug the real issues of human existence (damnation, salvation, the nature of sin, the nature of virtue, the whole problem of what constitutes reality; what is *really* real)—all these themes and concerns have come flooding into Western literature in the past two centuries.

Moreover, this idea, that real life emerges only in the lower depths, is one of the dominant themes of American culture and literature. Thus Whitman:

I take for my love some prostitute—I pick out some lower person for my dearest friend,
He shall be lawless, rude, illiterate—he shall be one condemned by others for deeds done.

Or Emerson: "I embrace the common, I explore and sit at the feet of the familiar, the low." Or Harold Frederic in *The Damnation of Theron Ware,* having Theron Ware describe his experience in the lower depths of New York (not at all unlike the province of *The Iceman*):

> I've been drinking for two days and one whole night, on my feet all the while, wandering alone in that big strange New York, going through places where they murdered men for ten cents, mixing myself up with the worst people in low bar-houses and dance houses, and they saw I had money in my pocket, too,—and yet nobody touched me, or offered to lay a finger upon me. Do you know why? They understood that I wanted to get drunk and couldn't. The Indians won't harm an idiot, or lunatic, you know. Well, it was the same with the vilest of the vile. They saw that I was a fool whom God had taken hold of, to break his heart first, and then to craze his brain, and then to fling him on a dunghill to die, like a dog. They believe in God, these people. They're the only ones who do, it seems to me.

In short, the lower down on the social scale, the more clearly and powerfully (so one may think) the elemental and basic issues of human experience emerge. Finally, as one peels away the layers of respectability, humanity itself begins to emerge. O'Neill himself felt an affinity to Gorky and on the occasion of Gorky's death he wrote:

> Gorki is not dead. His genius and his spirit of tragic understanding and pity for humanity which characterized his work will live as long as true literature is read.

3. The Form and the Language of The Iceman Cometh

The Iceman embodies formal elements that are both new departures for O'Neill, considering his career as a whole, and familiar elements. To take the familiar first: O'Neill's archetypal settings from first to last—there were exceptions, of course—were a middle-class home, a farm, a ship, and a bar. It is appropriate then that his last plays should have occurred, respectively, on a farm, with a bar in the background (*A Moon for the Misbegotten*); in a middle-class home by the sea, with a bar in the background (*Long Day's Journey*); in a combined home and bar (*A Touch of the Poet*); and in a bar (*The Iceman*). Further, it could be said that Harry Hope's saloon in *The Iceman* serves much the same function that the ship did in O'Neill's early sea plays. First, the ship was isolated and confined the characters, cutting them off from normal society, intensifying their own interrelationships, and making them in effect a society in themselves, a microcosmic reflection of the great world. So too, appropriately, in *The Iceman Cometh* Larry describes the isolation of the inhabitants of Hope's in sea imagery ("The Bottom of the Sea Rathskeller"):

> Don't you notice the beautiful calm in the atmosphere? That is because it's the last harbor. No one here has to worry about where they're going to next, because there is no farther they can go.

Similarly, the ship crews in the early plays constituted a racial "melting pot," replete with colorful contrasts, including verbal ones, and built-in tensions and interplay. By the same token a seedy bar in New York would have the same racial heterogeneity, and thus the same colorfulness, especially in the language.

Whether on shipboard or at home or in a bar, the primordial O'Neill situation is invariably men, and sometimes women, talking and drinking. In fact if alcohol were removed from his plays, many of the plays themselves would disintegrate. But the point to be made is that O'Neill does not describe the effects of alcohol realistically; rather drink in his plays is a formal device, every bit as much as the Elizabethan soliloquy, used to achieve certain effects. The unreality of the massive drinking that is supposedly going on in *The Iceman* is pointed out by Mary McCarthy. None of the characters, she says (she is describing a stage performance: see below), is visibly drunk;

no one has a hangover (this assertion is not true); with one exception (Oban) no one has the shakes; there are:

> . . . none of those rancorous, semi-schizoid silences, no obscurity of thought, no dark innuendoes, no flashes of hatred, there is, in short, none of the terror of drink . . . a form of insanity.

What precisely is missing, according to Miss McCarthy, is the final horror of drunkenness, the sense of the destruction of a personality; rather each character in the play is always in perfect possession of his or her own character.

Yet at the same time O'Neill is using with great skill many of the side-effects of alcohol for dramatic effects. It should also be remembered that even scientific opinion today is unsure as to the precise effects of alcohol, and that O'Neill's personal experience in these matters was considerable. Strong drink, first, is the way to oblivion, which is what the sinners and down-and-outers of *The Iceman* most urgently desire. Second, it cancels inhibitions and thus allows speeches of extraordinary candor. Third, alcohol is the great nostalgia-invoker as well, bringing back the past in a special way: roseate, simplified, happier than it really was, falsified, a little island in time that is warmer than the dreary desolation of present reality: the "pipe dream of yesterday." Again, alcohol can be, under certain conditions, exhilarating, not because it is a stimulant—actually it is a depressant—but because it blacks out certain levels of consciousness and can thus give rise to wild and sudden hilarity and to great expectations about the future: "the tomorrow movement." Further, O'Neill was acute enough to see that alcohol is never an absolute, producing always the same effect, but instead engenders a result which is relative to the state of mind or mood of the drinker. Thus when Hickey, the "truth-teller," begins his evangelical campaign to drag the denizens of Harry Hope's kicking and screaming into reality, alcohol becomes for all of them only a depressant: "Bejees, what did you do to the booze, Hickey?" "We can't pass out! You promised us peace!" But when Hickey leaves, "the booze" becomes benign once more.

Last but not least, alcohol puts one to sleep. Thus O'Neill is able to move the various members of his large cast in and out of the dramatic action, without any of the awkwardness or artificialities of repeated exits and entrances, by periodically letting them snooze at their tables.

Another primordial O'Neill formal device is the day-night, or night-day, cycle, with special emphasis on sunrise, sunset, and late or deep night; in short, the long day's journey into night. He had a habit as well of attaching certain meanings or moods to each of these crucial junctures. Dawn usually signifies reality, cold, austere, somber, inescapable. Thus Hickey, the bringer of reality, does not come on in Act I of *The Iceman* until Rocky has turned off the lights and the back room of Harry Hope's is lit by the dim light of dawn. Deep night usually signifies two contrasting things: oblivion and "truth-telling." Act IV of *The Iceman* embodies both: Hickey has told an ultimate truth, as has Larry when he tells Parritt to get out of life, but the rest of the characters sink into an alcoholic never-never land. As for the day itself, O'Neill usually chose, especially in the late plays, a hot and humid one so that his characters will suffer not only psychologically but physiologically as well. Hickey's "reform-movement" is thus peculiarly harsh because it involves sending these sodden alcoholics out into the blinding hot streets of New York at midmorning in midsummer. As Harry Hope says, "Too damned hot for a walk though, if you ask me."

The most important and consequential new formal device that O'Neill adopted in his late plays was the so-called "unities": of time, place, and action. In his first career O'Neill was in the habit, although not always, of employing great time spans and switching from place to place, thus, in effect, constructing narrative dramas: in *All God's Chillun Got Wings* some seventeen years; in *Strange Interlude* some twenty-seven or twenty-eight years and many different places. Whatever the merits of this dramatic method, and there are many, it lacks simply one of the great dramatic virtues, which *Oedipus Rex* classically and forever demonstrates—the concentration or unity of effect, compression, high and continuous emotional pressure—however one wishes to describe it—which the "unities" alone engender: one place, one brief stretch of time, and one continuous action.

In *Oedipus Rex* the crucial action, the killing of the father and the sexual embrace with the mother, has already occurred before the play begins. The "action" of the play then is retrospective, as Oedipus plunges down and back into the past to find the "unclean thing" who is polluting his city and who is, unbeknownst to him, himself. By the same token the crucial actions of *The Iceman,* Hickey's murder of his wife and Parritt's betrayal of his mother, have already occurred before the play opens. Although the audience of *The Iceman,* unlike the knowing audience of *Oedipus,* does not know until the end that Hickey is a murderer, it can soon guess that Parritt betrayed his mother and the parallel to *Oedipus* still holds on a psychological level, for both Hickey and Parritt are seeking to find what their real motivation was. As, at the end of *Oedipus,* the king discovers himself to be the great sinner, so at the end of *The Iceman* both Hickey and Paritt finally find out, or bring themselves at last to admit, the true motive for their actions, which was hatred.

The inner subject or working principle of *The Iceman Cometh* is the vagaries of the human memory—its tendency to rationalize the past, and its consequent inability to know what really happened. While nothing much occurs in the two day time span of the play, the real dynamics are provided by a protean past that keeps welling up and spilling over into the present. Each character must repeatedly make a backward journey, groping back into the past for the self he has lost. In each case the memory spews forth a compound of guilt and nostalgia, self-accusation and glorification—in short, distortion: thus Harry Hope can at times transform his shrew, Bessie, into a loving spouse. The future is really unthinkable in any realistic way, as Hickey forces them all to admit. The present—suspended, isolated, alcoholic—is unreal. Only the past is alive, dynamic, restless, unappeasable. With it, says *The Iceman Cometh,* we can never come to terms, and only death can end this infinite debate of self with self.

Two other aspects of the structure of *The Iceman Cometh* should be noted. The first is that the general movement of the play is from comedy to tragedy. O'Neill himself described it as "a big kind of comedy that doesn't stay funny very long" and thought that Act I was one of the funniest pieces he had ever written. The second aspect is O'Neill's practice of creating rather fully, two characters who never appear on the stage, Parritt's mother and Hickey's wife. Yet so fully drawn are they, the strong and domineering woman and the sweet, self-effacing one (now, of course, dead), that they hover over the play like ghosts as almost palpable embodiments of the spirit of memory that haunts the characters.

O'Neill and language make up a peculiar phenomenon. He is commonly described as a great "writer" who could not "'write" (see Mary McCarthy). While it is true that O'Neill's verbal gifts were not Shakespearean and while it is true that in many of his plays there are vast stretches of banal and overheated rhetoric, it should be remembered that one of his real distinctions as a playwright was that he brought into the American drama and onto the American stage the various idioms of the American vernacular. Prior to O'Neill, American stage dialogue had tended to be stilted and artificial. Thus it might be said that O'Neill did for the American drama what Mark Twain did for the American novel, or that, like Wordsworth with English poetry, he brought it back to reality: simple people saying simple things in a simple way but giving representation to the most genuine and elemental of human emotions. Moreover, with dialects O'Neill was somewhat of a virtuoso: Swedish, Irish brogue, American Negro, New England rural, among others, all appear under considerable control and with a high degree of authenticity in his plays. He thus used the variety of sub-educated dialects provided by American culture to compose what might be called linguistic "medleys," as he did with his

polyglot sailors in the early sea plays. But his largest and most comprehensive linguistic "symphony" is *The Iceman Cometh*: Rocky and
Chuck (lower-class New Yorkese); Larry (middle-class American with
an Irish flavor); Hugo (Hungarian-American); Willie Oban (middle-
class American); Harry (New York-Irish); Joe (Negro-American); Parritt (middle-class American); Lewis (English); Wetjoen (Dutch); Jimmy
(middle-class American with a Scottish flavor); McGloin and Mosher
(New York-Irish); Margie, Pearl, and Cora (New York lower class); and
Hickey (Mid-Western American salesman lingo, with an evangelical
flavor). O'Neill is in complete control of all of these accents, especially
their resources for humor. Thus in Act I, Rocky's speculations about
Chuck and Cora settling down, bucolically, to wedded bliss on a farm:

> What would gettin' married get dem? But de farm stuff is de sappiest
> part. When bot' of 'em was dragged up in dis ward and ain't never
> been nearer a farm dan Coney Island! Jees, dey'd tink dey'd gone deef
> if dey didn't hear de El rattle! Dey'd get D.T.'s if dey ever hoid a
> cricket choip! I hoid crickets once on my cousin's place in Joisey. I
> couldn't sleep a wink. Dey give me de heebie-jeebies. [*With deeper
> disgust*] Jees, can yuh picture a good barkeep like Chuck diggin' spuds?
> And imagine a whore hustlin' de cows home! For Christ sake! Ain't
> dat a sweet picture!
> MARGIE: [*rebukingly*] Yuh oughtn't to call Cora dat, Rocky. She's a good
> kid. She may be a tart, but—
> ROCKY: [*considerately*] Sure, dat's all I meant, a tart.
> PEARL: [*giggling*] But he's right about de damned cows, Margie. Jees, I
> bet Cora don't know which end of de cow has de horns! I'm goin' to
> ask her.

Or McGloin to his patron, Harry Hope: "It's not like you to be so
hard-hearted, Harry. Sure, it's hot, parching work laughing at your
jokes so early in the morning on an empty stomach!"

But the real test of dramatic dialogue is rather simple, on the face
of it, and consists in the continuous appropriateness of speech to
speaker. As Hugo Von Hofmannstahl pointed out in an early and
brilliant analysis of O'Neill's early plays, effective dialogue is not
dependent on "lyrical quality or rhetorical power":

> The best dramatic dialogue reveals not only the motives that determine
> what a character is to do—as well as what he tries to conceal—but suggests
> his very appearance, his metaphysical being as well as the grosser material
> figure. How this is done remains one of the unanswerable riddles of
> artistic creation. This suggestion of the "metaphysical" enables us to de-
> termine in an instant, the moment a person enters the room whether he
> is sympathetic or abhorrent, whether he brings agitation or peace; he
> affects the atmosphere about us, making it solemn or trivial, as the case
> may be.

So in *The Iceman* Parritt hardly opens his mouth before the audience knows he is a moral leper, "abhorrent"; and Hickey hardly opens his before the audience knows he is a walking ambiguity and that he brings "agitation," not "peace."

If O'Neill had any one principle, in addition to that of verisimilitude, in composing dialogue, it was a belief in the efficacy of repetition. O'Neill's concept here was musical and he thought of his verbal repetitions ("pipe dream" for example) as the "rhythm" of his plays, the leit-motifs that run through and bind up the whole. Not all his critics (see Eric Bentley below) agree with him on the efficacy of these repetitions. But he has had his defenders as well. The critic Stark Young said that in *Mourning Becomes Electra,* O'Neill "has come to what is so rare in Northern art, an understanding of the depth and subtlety that lie in repetition and variations on the same design." *Immortal Shadows* (N.Y. n.d.) p. 128.

4. The Themes of The Iceman Cometh

The only unequivocal statement about the nature of things in *The Iceman Cometh* is probably Larry's quizzical assertion in Act I:

> I was born condemned to be one of those who has to see all sides of a question. When you're damned like that, the questions multiply for you until in the end it's all question and no answer.

This same philosopher also pronounces the play's comment upon TRUTH:

> To hell with the truth! As the history of the world proves, the truth has no bearing on anything. It is irrelevant and immaterial, as the lawyers say.

At the same time, the play does explore the various enigmas by and within which men live, or try to live.

Philosophically considered, *The Iceman* is a parable analogous to the famous parable of the Cave in Plato's *Republic*. Plato's parable, which is about the nature of reality and man's relationship to it, describes the human condition as analogous to that of a group of prisoners chained to a wall in a cave, which is dimly lit by a fire. By the light of the fire they can see forms, their own and others, reflected on the wall. Thus all they can really see is their own shadows and the shadows of others; they give names to things but they are always misnaming, for they can never see anything but shadowy reflections. Outside of the cave, in the clear and unequivocal light of the sun, lies reality. Plato then describes how painful it would be for the prisoner if he were set free and forced to climb the steep ascent up out of the cave and out into the bright sun, which would dazzle him, and how he would resist the notion that what he had experienced in the cave was not the substance but merely the shadow, not reality but only illusion:

> Will he not fancy that the shadows which he formerly saw are truer than the objects which are now shown to him? [4]

Thus in Act III of *The Iceman* when the merciless but well-intentioned Hickey is forcing Harry Hope out into the bright sunshine of the New York streets, the old man exclaims, after Rocky has said it's a "fine day":

> What is that? Can't hear you. Don't look fine to me. Look's if it'd pour down cats and dogs any minute. My rheumatism—(*He catches himself*) No, must be my eyes. Half blind bijees. Makes things look black.

But here the analogy ends, for while in Plato's parable some men, the philosophers, finally emerge from the cave and stand straight in the sun and see the world for what it is, O'Neill's motley collection of derelicts finally scurry back into the alcoholic darkness of their "cave," Harry Hope's saloon.

One of the ambiguous pleasures of the darkened cave is that in it nothing is ever quite certain or clear-cut, even occupations and names. Thus nomenclature in *The Iceman Cometh* is both highly important and exceedingly problematical. The ambiguity and importance of nomenclature is carried throughout the play by two of its central running jokes: Larry as the old "Foolosopher" (fool and/or philosopher) and the question of whether Pearl and Margie are "tarts" or "whores." Names take on almost magical powers: you are what you are called, although what you are called may not be the truth about you. Furthermore there is a kind of crazy "logic" about names. They are like propositions in a scientific proof arranged in a chain of causation. Thus Pearl to Rocky: "Aw right, Rocky. We're whores, you know what dat makes you, don't you?" Margie: "A lousy little pimp, dat's what." Pearl: "A dirty little Ginny pimp, dat's what!" But when the reconciliation occurs at the end of the play, Rocky becomes once more, "Our little bartender" and "a cute little Ginny at dat!" Similarly Joe Mott is considered morally "'white,'" though "black" in color, in times of peace, but once Hickey's "cure" starts its dubious work he becomes a "dinge," a "black bastard," or "doity nigger." To Mott is given the single most ironical speech, concerning the problem of identity, in the play:

> Don't you get it in your heads I's pretending to be what I ain't, or dat I ain't proud to be what I is, get me?

[4] *The Republic*, Book VII, Jowett trans.

In the "Cave," then, nobody is quite sure who or what he is, but, unlike Plato, O'Neill suggests that perhaps life is more bearable that way.

So far as the play has an overall statable theme, it is concerned with two sets of distinct but connected antitheses: reality *vs.* illusion and commitment *vs.* noncommitment, with reality-commitment set off against illusion-noncommitment. Through most of the characters the play seems to say that man cannot face either reality or commitment but, through Larry, it suggests that he cannot escape from either of them. The case of Hickey, however, would appear to say that man cannot tell what the reality is and thus where his real commitment lies. Hickey's commitment in the play, the seemingly admirable and sensible and charitable mission of relieving his friends of their pipe dreams, their preoccupations with the past and the future, and all the concomitant guilts, is no less than a disaster for two reasons. First, the world does not work that way; in Larry's words ". . . the great nihilist, Hickey! He's started a movement that'll blow up the world!" Second, illusions about themselves are one of the saving graces of human beings and without this soothing balm people are liable to turn nasty and cynical, as do the characters of *The Iceman*. "No," says Larry to Rocky after refusing Rocky's offer to join him in business, "it doesn't look good, Rocky. I mean, the peace Hickey's brought you. It isn't contented enough, if you have to make everyone else a pimp, too."

The real province of *The Iceman Cometh* is that deep, tortuous, problematical territory of human nature where there are two final questions: how much guilt can a human being stand and how is he or she, no matter how degraded the circumstances, to preserve some shred or semblance or simulacrum of human dignity, however shabby? Though Man has been defined by Nietzsche as the "laughing animal," *The Iceman* would seem to lean to the Freudian proposition, that he is best described as the "guilty animal." Thus the play is, on the one hand, a vast exploration of degrees of guilt, from the easy-going complaisance of the "tarts" to the deep-dyed torment of Hickey and Parritt. But only Hickey and Parritt fall below zero on the moral scale. In them is embodied the grimmest implication of the play, namely that the capacity to bear guilt is not limitless but finite and its heaped-up totality can eventuate in murder. Thus Hickey:

> I even caught myself hating her for making me hate myself so much.
> There's a limit to the guilt that you can feel and the forgiveness and pity you can take.

So too Larry must finally tell Parritt what Parritt wishes to hear—that his guilt is too great and that he must die:

Go, for the love of Christ, you mad tortured bastard, for your own sake!

Betrayal of another human being would seem to be the ultimate destructive act, the sin against the Holy Ghost, and the unforgivable crime.

On the other hand, if the guilt is less than overwhelming, as is the case with most of the characters, then some kind of dignity, however specious, is a psychological necessity. O'Neill's own comment on his derelicts has already been quoted above: "In some queer way they carried on." Their "dignity," their ability to carry on, lies precisely in "the pipe dream" and thus follows their hatred of the man who will rob them of it. The gentlest and the most sensitive of all the characters (and one of the three Hickey wants most to "save," the others being Harry and Larry) is Jimmy Tomorrow. It makes sense then that his reaction to Hickey's plan is the most violent and the most out of character:

> JIMMY: [*in a burst of futile fury*] You Dirty swine! [*He tries to throw the drink in HICKEY'S face . . .*]

What Hickey does not realize is that all the "pipe dreamers" know full well that their own "'dreams" and those of their fellows are a sham but they have tacitly agreed to a conspiracy of "keeping up appearances" and of somehow carrying on. There is a profound psychological "truth" in this insight, even if, admittedly, it is shown in a gross and obvious fashion. Indeed it could be argued that society is held together, even in the highest circles, by some such mechanism of mutual forbearance for harmless delusions. The truth is terrible, says *The Iceman Cometh*: let us gloss it over, although we always know it is there.

But it is wrong perhaps to anatomize the play in this way, for certainly no simple moral emerges from it. Further, many of its concerns and themes are paradoxes: Is it more reprehensible to hide from reality than to face it? Does anybody really know what he or she is actually doing and why? Do we all secretly long for death or is death what we seek everlastingly to avoid? Is there such a thing as truth and if so, who has it or where is it? If we ever did get our heart's desires, would we be happy? How close are love and hate in intimate relationships and how does one tell one from the other? When we feel pity for the weaknesses and failures of others, are we helping them or hurting them? Who is sure of his own identity? What is concluded that we should reach any conclusions about it?

About the only thing that one can say with finality is that life has certain stages, that it is like a dream, and that it finally comes to an end. Thus Hugo: "So ve get drunk, and ve laugh like hell and den ve die, and de pipe dream vanish."

5. *The Reception of* The Iceman Cometh *and the Idea of an American Tragedy*

The Iceman Cometh was written in 1939, its composition coinciding with the outbreak of World War II. O'Neill was horrified by Hitler and had great sympathy for France, and some of the more pessimistic aspects of the play were no doubt inspired by the fact that Western civilization seemed to be on its way to holocaust and general destruction. He felt, too, later on, that the first production of the play should have a relationship to the War. Thus he told the Theatre Guild that *The Iceman Cometh* should not be produced immediately after the conclusion of the War. If the play were to be put on directly after the War was over, its pessimism would run counter to the public optimism consequent to the victory in the War. But he felt that in a year or so disillusionment would set in and that then the play would be properly appreciated. Accordingly, the play was not produced until 1946. (Three reviews, by George Jean Nathan, Rosamond Gilder, and Mary McCarthy are included below.) It was not an unqualified success—many people, for example, complained of its length. O'Neill's critical reputation, already on the decline, was probably not enhanced and may have been damaged further by the play. O'Neill himself confessed late in 1946 that he was "down in the dumps" and was thus grateful when he received a letter praising *The Iceman* from Tennessee Williams.

In 1956 in a small off-Broadway theatre-in-the-round, in a building that had once been a night-club and that could hold less than two hundred people, José Quintero, a then unknown director, staged a production of *The Iceman Cometh*. Whether it was the intimate setting or whether it was the director and the cast or whether it was the passage of time—for whatever reason—the play was an immediate success and went on for 565 performances. (See Brooks Atkinson's review below.) Today *The Iceman* appears to be, along with *Long Day's Journey Into Night*, the most substantial dramatic literature ever composed on this continent, to which the growing critical literature about it would attest.

One of the insistent impulses of American culture has been to attempt to take the old European forms of literature, notably the epic and the drama, and to translate them into the American grain, that is, to use indigenous materials, and to re-create the age-old heroic timbre and the age-old tragic timbre in terms of the American democ-

racy and the idea of the "melting pot." In *Moby Dick* Melville chal-
lenged the ancient epic in just these terms; of his motley ship's crew on
the "Pequod" he declared:

> If, then, to meanest mariners and renegades and castaways, I shall
> hereafter ascribe high qualities, though dark; weave round them tragic
> graces; if even the most mournful, perchance the most abased, among
> them all, shall at times lift himself to the exalted mounts; if I shall touch
> that workman's arm with some ethereal light; if I shall spread a rainbow
> over his disastrous set of sun; then against all mortal critics bear me out
> in it, thou just Spirit of Equality, . . .

O'Neill, attempting a similar metamorphosis in the realm of tragedy,
challenges the historical European notion of tragedy even more insistently. Traditionally, whether in *Oedipus Rex* or *King Lear,* high
tragedy involves the fall of a great man. But in *The Iceman Cometh*
all the men are little and all the falls have already taken place before
the play begins. In short, O'Neill is standing on its head the classic
concept of what constitutes "the tragic." For what he seems to be
saying is that *all* life, all human experience at all levels of society, is
tragic, though relieved at times by humor. This is the human condition, no matter where one looks. One cannot do better than to quote
O'Neill himself on what he was driving at in *The Iceman Cometh*:

> There is a feeling around, or I'm mistaken, of fate. Kismet, the negative
> fate; not in the Greek sense. . . . It's struck me as time goes on, how
> something funny, even farcical, can suddenly without any apparent
> reason, break up into something gloomy and tragic. . . . A sort of unfair
> *non sequitur,* as though events, as though life, were being manipulated
> just to confuse us. I think I'm aware of comedy more than I ever was
> before; a big kind of comedy that doesn't stay funny very long. I've made
> some use of it in *The Iceman.* The first act is hilarious comedy, *I think,*
> but then some people may not even laugh. At any rate, the comedy breaks
> up and the tragedy comes on. . . .

And the little men of *The Iceman* are all variations on Everyman.

PART ONE

View Points

Letters from O'Neill to Lawrence Langner

Later on, a mention in the newspapers about a new O'Neill play called *The Iceman Cometh* aroused our curiosity; the situation was explained fully by 'Gene in his letter of July 17, 1940:

> One reason I haven't sent you or Terry a script is that there are only two in existence. I have one and I sent the other to Bennett Cerf to lock in the Random House safe for safekeeping—but not for publication. Don't blame Bennett for not telling you or Terry. I made him promise to keep it dark from everyone, bar none. Frankly, I did not want you to see it yet —in New York. I was afraid you would want to produce it right away and I don't want the strain of any production now. There are other good reasons against it, too. On the other hand, if you or Terry happened out this way, as you thought you might, then I could give you the script to read with the proviso that production was out for the present, and do all my explaining why at the same time. But the idea of trying to do all this in letters simply had me stopped. Hence the secrecy. To tell the truth, like anyone else with any imagination, I have been absolutely sunk by this damned world debacle. The Cycle is on the shelf, and God knows if I can ever take it up again because I cannot foresee any future in this country or anywhere else to which it could spiritually belong.
>
> Well, to hell with that. I'm writing this to explain my past few months secrecy re the completion of *The Iceman Cometh,* and to say if you and Armina, Terry and Oliver, want to read this opus you can get the script from Bennett. I'm writing to release him from his pledge of secrecy as far as you and Terry are concerned. But give it back to Cerf to lock up in the safe afterwards, and *please don't* let anyone else see it. Remember only two scripts exist and it's no time to let too many people, even in the Guild, really know about it yet. And forget about any production.

*   *   *

Terry and I both read the new play, and felt it to be one of 'Gene's major works. 'Gene replied to my comments in a letter dated August 11, 1940:

> Many thanks for your letter regarding *The Iceman Cometh.* I'm damned pleased you liked it so well. Personally, I love it! And I'm sure

From "O'Neill and The Iceman Cometh" *in* The Magic Curtain, *by Lawrence Langner (New York: E. P. Dutton & Co., 1951), pp. 397-98. Copyright © 1951 by Lawrence Langner. Reprinted by permission of Armina M. Langner.*

my affection is not wholly inspired by nostalgia for the dear dead days "on the bottom of the sea," either! I have a confident hunch that this play, as drama, is one of the best things I've ever done. In some ways, perhaps *the* best. What I mean is, there are moments in it that suddenly strip the secret soul of a man stark naked, not in cruelty or moral superiority, but with an understanding compassion which sees him as a victim of the ironies of life and of himself. Those moments are for me the depth of tragedy, with nothing more that can possibly be said.

Letter from O'Neill to Barrett Clark, Sept., 1943

. . . When, in addition, I consider *The Iceman Cometh*, most of which was written after war started in '39, and *Long Day's Journey Into Night*, written the following year—(these two plays give me greater satisfaction than any other two I've ever done)—and a one-act play, *Hughie*, one of a series of eight I want to do under the general title, *By Way of Obit*, I feel I've done pretty well in the four war years. I go into the above details to assure you that, until lately, I have not been upset by war, sickness, or anything else to the point where I have quit on my job.

Letter and Interview from "Temporary Retirement" in Eugene O'Neill: The Man and His Plays, *by Barrett H. Clark (New York: Dover Publications, Inc., 1947), pp. 147, 151. Copyright 1929, renewal © 1957 by Barrett H. Clark. Reprinted by permission of the publisher.*

Interview with O'Neill by Barrett Clark, March, 1943

. . . And then he talked about *The Iceman Cometh*. He gave me a set of proofs, and said he thought I would like the play. "Mere physical violence—mere bigness, is not important. You'll see that *The Iceman* is a very simple play: one set; I've certainly observed the Unities all right, characterization, but no plot in the ordinary sense; I didn't need plot: the people are enough."

Croswell Bowen on the rehearsals of *The Iceman Cometh*

Readings of *The Iceman Cometh* began in May. James Barton was cast in the role of Harry Hope. O'Neill was impressed with Barton's

Excerpted from the chapter "Past and Present: The Iceman Cometh" in Curse of the Misbegotten, *by Croswell Bowen (New York: McGraw-Hill Book Company, 1959), pp. 309-10. Copyright © 1959 by Croswell Bowen. Reprinted by permission of the publisher.*

sensitive reading of the part. It was now a new play to O'Neill; it was always this way when he heard one of his plays read for the first time. Throughout the summer of 1946, the Theatre Guild, the cast and the playwright worked on the rehearsals. Everyone knew that in a sense the play would constitute a kind of reopening of the Broadway theatre after the war. It would be like old times—another O'Neill play on Broadway.

There was more pressure exerted on O'Neill than ever before to get him to cut the play. Langner gave him a copy of the play with passages marked where, in the producer's opinion, cuts were very much indicated. In a blue pencil O'Neill wrote boldly the word "no" opposite most of them. When he wrote "yes" it was in a tiny, faltering script. On the cover of the manuscript he handed back to Langner, he wrote: "The hell with your cuts! E.O'N."

In September, as the rehearsals came closer to being finished performances, Paul Crabtree, one of the actors, studied the script and figured out that O'Neill had made the same point eighteen times. He showed the fruits of his research to Langner who, he reckoned, would have the nerve to raise the point—or rather, the eighteen repeated points—with O'Neill. Langner has set down O'Neill's exact reaction: Gene looked at me and replied in a particularly quiet voice, "I intended to be repeated eighteen times!" Langner then observed that *The Iceman Cometh,* like Shaw's *Saint Joan,* would never be properly produced until the copyright had expired. Again O'Neill smiled. "It will have to wait," he said, "for just that."

Often the rehearsals of an O'Neill play would degenerate into a series of running battles between the playwright and the producer, the director, and the actors. Invariably, O'Neill was able to stand his ground against them all.

A typical dispute during the rehearsals of *The Iceman Cometh* concerned the play's length, which seemed inordinate to several members of the company. When all other arguments failed, someone came to O'Neill and told him that the play was running at least twenty minutes too long and that a cut would have to be made. Why? O'Neill asked. It was then patiently explained to the author that the last commuting trains would have left Grand Central Station before the audience even got out of the theatre.

O'Neill indicated succinctly that he was interested only in the play, not in whether the audience caught their trains. It was his play, and it would be done his way.

But as the rehearsals proceeded, the cast's affection and respect for O'Neill mounted. He knew the theatre and he knew his play, and the actors were aware that he was part of America's theatrical heritage. Most of the time, O'Neill sat next to Eddie Dowling, the director.

Dowling, O'Neill felt, tended to encourage the players to overplay their parts. The cast wanted to get the full implications of the play, its shadings and meanings, and O'Neill was always ready to explain his characters for the actors.

"Raw emotion," O'Neill said, "produces the worst in people. Remember, goodness can surmount anything. The people in that saloon were the best friends I've ever known . . . Their weakness was not an evil. It is a weakness found in all men."

O'Neill tried to explain to the cast the meaning behind the extraordinary behavior of the habitués of the saloon—the meaning behind their deeply troubled words.

"Revenge," he said, "is the subconscious motive for the individual's behavior with the rest of society. Revulsion drives a man to tell others of his sins . . . It is the Furies within us that seek to destroy us.

"In all my plays sin is punished and redemption takes place.

"Vice and virtue cannot live side by side. It's the humiliation of a loving kiss that destroys evil."

An eager, aggressive actor asked O'Neill where he stood on "the labor movement." (Two of the characters in the play are disillusioned radicals.)

"I am a philosophical anarchist," O'Neill said, smiling faintly, "which means, 'Go to it, but leave me out of it.' "

Interview with O'Neill by J. S. Wilson

"I'm going on the theory that the United States, instead of being the most successful country in the world, is the greatest failure," O'Neill said, seemingly grateful to have something to talk about. "It's the greatest failure because it was given everything, more than any other country. Through moving as rapidly as it has, it hasn't acquired any real roots. Its main idea is that everlasting game of trying to possess your own soul by the possession of something outside of it, thereby losing your own soul and the thing outside of it, too. America is the prime example of this because it happened so quickly and with such immense resources. This was really said in the Bible much better. We are the greatest example of 'For what shall it profit a man, if he shall gain the whole world, and lose his own soul?' We had so much and could have gone either way."

This attitude of O'Neill's is not confined simply to the United States. It spreads to all humanity.

From PM, *Sept. 3, 1946, p. 18. Report by John S. Wilson of* PM *on an interview with O'Neill at the Theatre Guild Offices, Sept. 2, 1946.*

"If the human race is so damned stupid," he said, "that in 2000 years it hasn't had brains enough to appreciate that the secret of happiness is contained in one simple sentence which you'd think any grammar school kid could understand and apply, then it's time we dumped it down the nearest drain and let the ants have a chance. That simple sentence is: 'What shall it profit a man?'

*   *   *

The ice man in the title, he said, had a twofold meaning. The chief character is a salesman. There is the salesman's old story that when he is stewed he would go sobbing around from table to table in bars, hauling out a picture of his wife and blubbering about "my poor wife." "But she's safe," the salesman would say. "I left her in bed with the ice man."

"That is a superficial meaning of the title," O'Neill said. "It also has a deeper meaning connected with death."

*   *   *

He was asked which of his plays he liked best.

"That is really two questions," he parried. "It should be which play I like best and which play I *think* is best. I like *The Hairy Ape.* As for which one I think is best—well, *The Ice Man* is just coming on, so—" He spread his hands and smiled. "But really," he added, "I love *The Ice Man.*"

Comment by O'Neill reported by Rosamond Gilder, Sept. 5, 1946

. . . Miss Gilder reports, in her radio broadcast, *The American Theatre in Review* (Sept. 5), that at the same interview "a youngster" asked O'Neill, "How can one learn to be a playwright?" O'Neill "looked at his interlocutor for a long moment and then said very quietly: 'Take some wood and canvas and nails and things. Build yourself a theater, a stage, light it, learn about it. When you've done that you will probably know how to write a play—that is to say if you can.' " This, I take it, was not a flippant remark. Is it necessary to add that the experienced playwright was here advising a beginner to re- member that what he has to show and say must be conveyed in terms of physical theater?

From Eugene O'Neill: The Man and His Plays, *by Barrett Clark (New York: Dover Publications, Inc., 1947), p. 153. Copyright © 1926 by Barrett Clark. Re- printed by permission of the publisher.*

Interview with O'Neill by S. J. Woolf

. . . When I asked him how long a play should be he said: "As long
as necessary to tell the story. No play is too long that holds the interest of its audience. If a short play is tiresome it is too long and
if a long play is absorbing until the fall of the last curtain no one
will pull out his watch to look at the time."

*   *   *

Most of O'Neill's talk, while I was sketching, was of the theatre, and
much of it was reminiscent. Several times he mentioned his father, the
celebrated James O'Neill. As a child, the playwright traveled widely
with the elder O'Neill's troupe. "Almost the first words of my father I
remember," he said, "are, 'The theatre is dying.' And those words
seem to me as true today as when he said them. But the theatre must
be a hardy wench, for although she is still ailing, she will never die
as long as she offers an escape."

*   *   *

It was no surprise that a dramatist who has consistently written
"experimental" plays should talk at length about theatre technique.
New techniques, O'Neill pointed out, often amount to no more than
fads. He mentioned expressionism as one fad that had waxed and
waned in the modern theatre, and while he poked fun at that movement's excesses, he was quick to add that it had had "some good influence in playwriting. The trouble with a fad—and this holds true
for any form of art—is that it affords an opportunity for people who
do not know the technique to pose as artists. There are as well-estab-
lished rules for the theatre as there are for painting and music. The
only ones who can successfully break the rules are the people who
know them. A knowledge of rules is necessary, even if adhering to
tradition is not."

*   *   *

He sat still for some minutes, saying nothing and staring out into
space. In one of his thin hands was the ever-present cigarette—a mild
brand with a cork tip and cotton filter. His thoughts seemed far away
and I hesitated to break the silence. Suddenly he looked up and a

"Interview with O'Neill by S. J. Woolf" from **The New York Times Magazine**
*(September 15, 1946), pp. 11, 61, 62. Copyright © 1946 by The New York Times
Company. Reprinted by permission of the publisher and Muriel Woolf Hobson.*

smile spread over his face. He said that he had been thinking of the
past.

He added: "I am not saying that some of the actors and actresses
who interpreted my plays did not add something to them. But, after
all, even an owl thinks her owlets are the most beautiful babies in the
world and that's the way an author feels about his stage children. It
is for this reason that I always attend the rehearsals of my plays. While
I do not want to change the personalities of the artists acting in them,
I want to make it clear to them what was in my mind when I wrote
the play.

"I confess, though, that I have never been completely satisfied with
anything that I have done and I constantly rewrite my plays until they
are produced and even then I always see things which I could improve
and I regret that it is too late to make more changes.

"For, after all, anyone who creates anything must feel deeply. Like
Shaw, he may cover up his sincerity with humor, he may make light
of his efforts, but those efforts are nevertheless heart-breaking."

Interview with O'Neill by Karl Schriftgriesser

"I knew 'em all," he said. "I've known 'em all for years." His voice
dropped gropingly into his remembrance of things past. "All these
people I have written about, I once knew." Another long pause. "I do
not think that you can write anything of value or understanding about
the present. You can only write about life if it is far enough in the
past. The present is too much mixed up with superficial values; you
can't know which thing is important and which is not.

"The past which I have chosen is one I knew. The man who owns
this saloon, Harry Hope, and all the others—the Anarchists and Wobblies and French Syndicalists, the broken men, the tarts, the bartenders and even the saloon itself—are real. It's not just one place, perhaps, but it is several places that I lived in at one time or another"—
he let his brooding eyes wander over the present living room, with its
books and comfortable furniture, and his beloved collection of rec-
ords neatly stacked on shelves—"places I once knew put together in
one.

"What have I done with this setting? Well, I've tried to show the
inmates of Harry Hope's saloon there with their dreams. Some, you
see, have just enough money from home to keep them going; but
most of 'em keep from starving with the aid of the free lunch. This

"Interview with O'Neill by Karl Schriftgriesser" from The New York Times,
*Sunday Drama Section (October 6, 1946) pp. 1, 3. Copyright © 1946 by The New
York Times Company. Reprinted by permission of the publisher.*

old Tammany politician who runs the place lives with his dreams, too, and he loves these people for he is one of them in his way.

"You ask, what is the significance, what do these people mean to us today? Well, all I can say is that it is a play about pipe dreams. And the philosophy is that there is always one dream left, one final dream, no matter how low you have fallen, down there at the bottom of the bottle. I know, because I saw it."

*   *   *

. . . Its philosophy is eternal and universal, O'Neill thinks: "It will take man," he says, "a million years to grow up and obtain a soul."

O'Neill talked, too, about the title. To him titles are a matter of great importance.

"I always try to get into the title the surface meaning and at the same time the deeper significance."

The surface meaning of "The Iceman Cometh" stems from a sardonic wisecrack, often repeated by one of the characters, who tells people he has left his wife safe at home with the iceman. The play revolves around this. But as it proceeds the "iceman," who started as a ribald joke, takes on a different, deeper and even terrifying meaning and before the end becomes Death itself.

The idea for "Iceman" came to him suddenly. Because he knew all the characters so well there "was not so much hard work as if I had had to dig them out." Once started, the work "flowed right along, page after page," he recalled, his deep eyes happy with the memory. Later he revised it once.

"The Iceman Cometh" apparently was created more easily than others of his plays. "I don't just write plays," he explained. "I make many notes over a long period. Then I write a scenario of 20,000 or so words. I draw out all the scenes from my own strange conception of perspective, which I understand, even if directors don't always."

Review of the 1946 production of *The Iceman Cometh* by George Jean Nathan

With the appearance of *The Iceman Cometh,* our theatre has become dramatically alive again. It makes most of the plays of other American playwrights produced during the more than twelve-year period of O'Neill's absence look comparatively like so much damp

"*Review of the 1946 production of* The Iceman Cometh," *by George Jean Nathan. From* The Theatre Book of the Year, 1946-1947 *(New York: Alfred A. Knopf, Inc., 1947), pp. 93-96, 110-11. Copyright © 1947 by George Jean Nathan. Reprinted by permission of Mrs. Julie Haydon Nathan.*

tissue paper. In it there is an understanding of the deeper elements of human nature, a comprehension of the confused instincts that make up the life of mortals, and an evocation of pity for the tortured existence of dazed mankind that not merely most but all of those plays in combination have not faintly suggested. It is, in short, one of the best of its author's works and one that again firmly secures his position not only as the first of American dramatists but, with Shaw and O'Casey, one of the three really distinguished among the world's living.

These, I appreciate, are big words and probably contributive to the suspicion that their inditer has forgone his old Phyrronism. They are also doubtless obnoxious and challenging to such persons as either resent what seems to be extravagant praise at the expense of other playwrights or are constitutionally averse to superlatives of any kind and ready to throw off their coats if anyone has the gall to say even that Bach was the greatest composer who ever lived or that horseradish sauce is the best of all things to go with boiled beef. But the words, I believe, are none the less in good order. If they are not and if the play is not what I think it is, I am prepared to atone for my ignorance by presenting gratis to anyone who can offer convincing contrary evidence the complete bound works of all our American playwrights from Bronson Howard through Charles Klein, David Belasco and Augustus Thomas down to the geniuses responsible for *Joan of Lorraine, Another Part of the Forest, Dream Girl,* and *Maid in the Ozarks.*

Laying hold of an assortment of social outcasts quartered in a disreputable saloon on the fringe of New York in the year 1912 and introducing into their drunken semblance of contentful hope an allergy in the shape of a Werlean traveling salesman, O'Neill distils from them, slowly but inexorably, the tragedy that is death in life. Superficially at times suggesting a cross between Gorki's *The Lower Depths* and Saroyan's *The Time of Your Life,* let alone Ibsen's *The Wild Duck,* the play with its author's uncommon dramaturgical skill gradually weaves its various vagrant threads into a solid thematic pattern and in the end achieves a purge and mood of compassion that mark it apart from the bulk of contemporary drama. There are repetitions in the middle sections which O'Neill has deemed necessary to the impact of the play but which in this opinion might be got rid of with no loss. There is also still an excess of profanity, for all the author's liberal cutting, that becomes disturbing to any ear that gags at such overemphasis. And since the uncut version of *Hamlet,* which is a good play too, can be played in its entirety in little more than three and a half hours, the longer running time of *The Iceman Cometh* may seem to some, and quite rightly, not only superfluous but a little pretentious. Yet small matter. In the whole history of drama there has been only one really perfect tragedy—incidentally, only one-third as long—and, while this of O'Neill's is scarcely to be compared with it, it still rises far above its possible errors.

With a few nimble strokes, O'Neill pictures vividly the innards of even the least of his variegated characters, from the one-time circus grifter to the one-time police lieutenant, from the quondam boss of a Negro gambling den to the erstwhile Boer War correspondent, and from the night and day bartenders and the wreck of a college graduate to the former editor of Anarchist magazines and the old captain once in the British armed services. Only in the characters of his three street-walkers does he work rather obviously; truthfully, perhaps, but in a theatrically routine manner. Yet in his major figures, Slade, the one-time Syndicalist-Anarchist, Hickey, the hardware salesman, Hope, the proprietor of the saloon, etc., the hand is as steady and sure as ever.

The long monologue, only now and then momentarily interrupted, wherein toward the drama's conclusion the salesman relates the relief from himself secured by the murder of his wife, is one of the most impressive pieces of writing in contemporary dramatic literature: emotionally searching and definitely moving. The relations of Slade and the young man with memory of his betrayed mother on his agonized conscience are maneuvered with high suspensive dexterity, even if at one or two points to the hypercritical slightly overplanted. The dialogue throughout is driving; there is robust humor to alleviate the atmospheric sordidness; and out of the whole emerges in no small degree the profound essences of authentic tragedy.

In the author's own analysis of his play as he has confided it to me the dominant intention has been a study in the workings of strange friendship. That intention, it is not to be gainsaid, has been fully realized. But as I read the script and see it in stage action it seems to me that, far above and beyond it, there rises the theme of the tragedy which lies in bogus self-substantiation and the transient, pitiable satisfaction which it bequeaths. That, however, is the play's virtue: to different men it may convey different things. But to all with any emotional understanding and to all with any appreciation of the drama it must convey the satisfaction of a theatre that, if only for a short while, has again come into its rightful own.

*   *   *

He is a stickler for casting and direction. As to the latter, his constant concern is any sentimentalization of his work. "Where sentiment exists," he says, "there is sufficient of it in the characters, and any directional emphasis would throw it out of all proportion and make it objectionable." As to casting, he is generally opposed to so-called name actors. "They distract attention from the play to themselves," he argues. "My plays are not for stars but for simply good actors. Besides,

you can never count on the idiosyncrasies of stars; they may not stick
to a play and may so damage its chances on the road. I'm afraid of
them, as I've had some experience with them. Also, they sometimes
want you to change certain things in your play. Not for me!"

To return, finally, to *The Iceman Cometh,* I have already twice
remarked that it may very roughly be described as a kind of American
The Lower Depths. Like that play of Gorki's, though it in few other
ways resembles it, it treats of a group of degenerate outcasts and the
advent among them of a man with a philosophy of life new and disturbing to them. Its language is realistic, at times over-violently so;
its cast of alcoholic down-and-outs includes gamblers, grafting cops,
circus lot sharpers, whores, pimps, Anarchist riff-raff, military failures,
college-educated wastrels, stool-pigeons, *et al.;* and it is written in four
parts. It attests again to the fact, lost upon some of O'Neill's critics,
that he is far from lacking a healthy sense of humor. Some of the comedy writing is irresistible. It also demonstrates again the most barbed
appreciation of character known to any of his American playwriting
contemporaries. And it embraces, among many other things, the most
pitifully affecting picture of a woman—the unseen wife of the protagonist—that I, for one, have encountered in many years of playgoing.

Among the criticisms of the play is the argument that the characters
"do not grow." That they do not grow is O'Neill's specific dramatic
theme. Human beings sometimes change but change is not necessarily
growth. Change is frequently impermanent and retrogressive rather
than advancing as O'Neill indicates. Another argument is that Hickey,
the salesman of Death, in the end "explains himself with a textbook
clarity that robs him of a truly dramatic role in the play, or a really
human complexity." What of Nina in *The Sea Gull?* And a third con-
descendingly observes, "As for O'Neill's 'thesis,' it would seem to be
that men cannot live without illusions; hardly a new or very disputable idea." Hardly new, granted; but not very disputable? Come, come.
What of the sufficient disputations on occasion of Ibsen, Strindberg,
Zola, Hauptmann, Tolstoi, Wedekind, Shaw . . . ?

Rosamond Gilder: *"The Iceman Cometh"*

Like Peer Gynt's onion, the story of *The Iceman* has its layers and
layers of meaning. It touches on a dozen different themes and relationships. While the subsidiary characters are separate microcosms of

From "The Iceman Cometh," *by Rosamond Gilder, in* Theatre Arts Anthology
*(New York: Theatre Arts Books, 1950), pp. 664-65. Copyright 1946 by Theatre Arts,
Inc. Copyright 1950 by Theatre Arts Books. Reprinted by permission of Theatre
Arts Books, N.Y.*

despair, the three chief figures, Hickey, Larry, and Parritt, are three aspects of man—each element loving and loathing the other. The play is in a very special sense a summary of much of O'Neill's past writing. Superficially it goes back as far as the vigorous sea plays with which he made his debut. Its frank barroom talk, its conventional tarts, its amiable drunks, its passion and violence are reminders of the impact of his first writing. Don Parritt, the boy rejected by his mother, haunted by the guilt of his betrayal of her, which is nothing less than matricide, recalls O'Neill's days of absorption in psychoanalysis while Larry the philosopher is the O'Neill who attempted a detachment and objectivity never native to him.

But it is through Hickey who has known the love that passeth understanding and has rejected it that we glimpse O'Neill's ultimate meaning. Blind, besotted, and misguided, man haunted by death lives by lies. "The lie of a pipe dream is what gives life to the whole misbegotten mad lot of us, drunk or sober," Larry says at the opening of the play. But there is a truth which is not the truth of alcohol or political shibboleths, or psychology or philosophy, or even the truth of "facing the truth" which Hickey preaches. The greatest illusion of all is to believe that disillusionment—the unaided processes of the intellect—can solve man's dilemma. There is a force that, like the love that Hickey's wife bore him, is made of understanding and forgiveness. Man finds such love intolerable. "I couldn't forgive her for forgiving me," Hickey explains. "I caught myself hating her for making me hate myself so much. There is a limit to the guilt you can feel and the forgiveness and pity you can take." And so man denies, destroys and blasphemes such love, only in the end to find that this too will be forgiven. The denizens of Hickey's world and of the world at large find a simple answer to Hickey's final revelation. The man is mad! Hamlet to the contrary notwithstanding, there is nothing more in heaven and earth than can be compassed in any current philosophy. Pass the bottle. Drink up. What the hell! It's a good play, brother, why bother?

And it is a good play, excellently acted and directed, full of substance. It would seem that it could readily be compressed into a more reasonable running time, but O'Neill has a tendency to shirk the task of selection and condensation. He has so much to say that even this four-and-a-half-hour play must seem short to a man who thinks in terms of trilogies and nine-play cycles. For the onlooker, however, a shorter play would have brought into sharper focus the conflicting and merging elements of the three chief figures of the fable. The subsidiary characters are not sufficiently important or rounded to demand the time and attention they absorb. They are each set in their groove in the first half hour. They never emerge from the pattern to take on human proportions. The reiterated pattern of their false redemption and its death-dealing effect becomes tedious. Mr. O'Neill seems to underestimate the ability of the audience to grasp his idea, or perhaps more truly he has so fond a remembrance softened by time and distance of these denizens of his kingdom of despair that he cannot bear to tear up the sketches he has made in his mind's eye as he sat with them at marble-topped tables or leaned against mahogany bars in a hundred saloons the world over.

But the length of *The Iceman,* though it adds very little to the characterizations so boldly sketched in the first scenes, does permit an interesting orchestration of effects which Mr. Dowling has developed in this direction. The stage is almost continuously peopled by all the characters in the play at once. There is little movement; there is only an antiphonal development of themes. Besides the pipe-dream motive, which is developed in turn by each of the characters playing in groups of threes and fours, there is also the predominant, haunting theme of Death. O'Neill's bums are all in pursuit of forgetfulness, of sleep, of death. They spend most of their time in blissful or tormented alcoholic slumber. O'Neill uses this device to bring them in and out of the action without making them leave the stage. As the play progresses, the way the tables are grouped in the backroom and bar and the manner in which actors are grouped around them—slumped over asleep or sitting in a deathly daydream—provides a constant visual comment on the developing theme.

José Quintero: "Postscript to a Journey"

On March 15, 1956, I went to see Carlotta Monterey O'Neill for the first time, to discuss a possible revival of her late husband's tragedy *The Iceman Cometh.*

The Circle in the Square Theatre, of which I am director and one of the producers, had been yearning to do a work by Eugene O'Neill for a long time. But whenever we made inquiries we always met the same answer, "All the works of Mr. O'Neill, are, at the moment, not available for production." Mrs. O'Neill's invitation to call seemed promising, and I was a hopeful, if anxious, visitor. I was frightened and nervous, for my hostess was, after all, the widow of America's greatest dramatist. It was a remarkable and, as it turned out, a portentous meeting. I saw a lady of medium height, her black hair pulled back and cut short at the back of the neck. The dark penetrating eyes

From "Postscript to a Journey," by José Quintero, in Theatre Arts, XLI (*April, 1957*), 27-29, 88. Copyright © by Theatre Arts Books, Inc. Reprinted by permission of Theatre Arts.

were arresting in the steadiness of their gaze. She was dressed in black, which she wore with distinction.

She began to talk about her husband's work, almost as though he were present, as in a sense he was. There were pictures of Eugene O'Neill everywhere. Pictures of him when he was a young, lean, handsome man. Other pictures when pain and anger and frustration had given his eyes a terrifying look. Pictures of Mr. and Mrs. O'Neill taken on their honeymoon in Paris. In the bookcases there were three or four copies of every one of his plays. Mrs. O'Neill talked of his dedication to his work, and how work was the only thing that he really cared about. She asked me a few questions about the Circle in the Square, and I answered them. She rose from her chair and said, "You can do *The Iceman Cometh.*" I left the apartment, almost believing that permission to do the play had come from the dead dramatist himself.

It was less a permission than a sacred charge. *The Iceman Cometh* presented enormous problems at the Circle. It has a cast of twenty, and almost every role is highly complex. The central part of Hickey the salesman, is one of the longest and most difficult in American theatre literature. Where was our little theatre going to get all of those people . . . on so stringently limited a budget? We sent out a casting call and began listening to actors, 100 to 125 a day. After four weeks we had cast all of the characters—with the exception of Hickey. It was an oddly assorted and most unorthodox cast, ranging from highly trained and experienced actors to ones who were beginning their careers at the age of fifty. Some of them had never been in a play before.

The impossible problem remained: We needed a great actor who would be willing to play for $30 a week. That was when Jason Robards, Jr. came into our lives. I had called him, really, with a lesser role in mind, but he insisted on reading a section of Hickey's big speech at the end of the play. (He later told me that he had needed a couple of drinks to make such a demand.)

We had found the impossible. We had found the actor for Hickey.

My approach in directing *The Iceman Cometh* was different from that used in any play I had ever done. It had to be, for this was not built as an orthodox play. It resembles a complex musical form, with themes repeating themselves with slight variation, as melodies do in a symphony. It is a valid device, though O'Neill has often been criticized for it by those who do not see the strength and depth of meaning the repetition achieves.

My work was somewhat like that of an orchestra conductor, emphasizing rhythms, being constantly aware of changing tempos; every character advanced a different theme. The paradox was that for the first time as a director, I began to understand the meaning of precision in drama—and it took a play four and one-half hours long to teach me, a play often criticized as rambling and overwritten.

We rehearsed four weeks and our opening took place on the afternoon of May 8, 1956. We didn't know then, of course, what the critics and the public would think; but at the end of that first performance we, all of us, had a sense of one important success; that a great play had won the right to be revaluated.

Review of the 1956 production of *The Iceman Cometh* by Brooks Atkinson

Since José Quintero's productions at Circle in the Square are always admirable, no one should be surprised by his latest achievement.

But it is impossible not to be excited by his production of Eugene O'Neill's *The Iceman Cometh,* which opened in Mr. Quintero's theatre yesterday. It is a major production of a major theatre work. Taking a long script with a massive theme, Mr. Quintero has succeeded in bringing every part of it alive in the theatre. Although he tells the story simply and spontaneously, he leaves no doubt about the value he places on O'Neill's place in the literature of the stage. Mr. Quintero seems to take him on the level of Ibsen, Strindberg, Gorky, and other modern masters of tragic writing.

If *The Iceman Cometh* seems to belong in Mr. Quintero's theatre, there is a good reason. For Circle in the Square was a night-club originally, and all four of the acts of the O'Neill drama are set in a saloon. The audience has the sensation of participating. The rows of seats are only an extension of David Hayes' setting of the battered, blowzy waterfront saloon and flophouse that is under the fabulous proprietorship of Harry Hope. A few tables and chairs, a squalid bar, a flimsy door leading into the street, a handful of fly-blown chandeliers and a few ranks of benches for the audience—they are all part of the same setting and closely related on that account.

In the circumstances, it is difficult to be objective about this melancholy, sardonic drama that pulls the rug from under the whole structure of life. It seems, not like something written, but like something that is happening. Although it is terrible in its comment on the need for illusions to maintain an interest in life, it is also comic. Some of the dialogue is pretty funny. On the surface, all the characters are comic, since they live in a world of befuddled fantasy and talk big to compensate for the puniness of their spirits.

Review of the 1956 production of The Iceman Cometh, *by Brooks Atkinson. From* The New York Times, *May 9, 1956. Copyright © 1956 by The New York Times Company. Reprinted by permission of the publisher.*

But beneath them there is nothing more substantial than a void of
blackness. These are creatures that once were men—very pungent and
picturesque creatures, too, for O'Neill was a good deal of a romantic.
But the tone of *The Iceman Cometh* is devastatingly tragic. Life is bearable, it seems to say, only when men contrive not to look at the truth.

The performance lasts four and three-quarter hours. For *The Iceman
Cometh* is one of the O'Neill marathon dramas. No doubt it could be
cut and compressed without destroying anything essential. But as a
creative work by a powerful writer, it is entitled to its excesses, which,
in fact, may account for the monumental feeling of doom that it pulls
down over the heads of the audience.

The performance is a vital one. Mr. Quintero is a versatile conductor who knows how to vary his attack with changes in volume and
rhythm; he knows how to orchestrate a performance. In one important
respect, this performance surpasses the original of ten years ago. Jason
Robards, Jr. plays Hickey, the catalyst in the narrative, like an evan-
gelist. His unction, condescension and piety introduce an element of
moral affection that clarifies the perspective of the drama as a whole.
His heartiness, his aura of good fellowship give the character of
Hickey a feeling of evil mischief it did not have before.

*   *   *

In both the writing and the acting, *The Iceman Cometh* is a mighty
theatre work. O'Neill is a giant, and Mr. Quintero is a remarkably
gifted artist.

Dudley Nichols on *The Iceman Cometh*

"The iceman of the title is, of course, death," Nichols observed. "I
don't think O'Neill ever explained, publicly, what he meant by the use
of the archaic word, 'cometh,' but he told me at the time he was writing
the play that he meant a combination of the poetic and biblical 'Death
cometh'—that is, cometh to all living—and the old bawdy story, a
typical Hickey [and Jamie O'Neill] story, of the man who calls upstairs,
'Has the iceman come yet?' and his wife calls back, 'No, but he's
breathin' hard.' Even the bawdy story is transformed by the poetic
intention of the title, for it is really Death which Hickey's wife, Evelyn,
has taken to her breast when she marries Hickey, and her insistence on
her great love for Hickey and his undying love for her and her death-
like grip on his conscience—her insistence that he *can* change and not

From O'Neill, *by Arthur and Barbara Gelb (New York: Harper & Row, Publishers, 1960), pp. 831-32, 877. Copyright © 1960 by Arthur and Barbara Gelb. Reprinted by permission of the authors.*

get drunk and sleep with whores—is making Death breathe hard on
her breast as he approaches ever nearer—as he is about 'to come' in
the vernacular sense. It is a strange and poetic intermingling of the
exalted and the vulgar, that title."

The truth of the play, as O'Neill explained to Nichols and to two
or three other close friends, was that Hickey had long ago begun to
harbor a murderous hatred for his wife; she represented his own,
punishing conscience.

"God, how Hickey had begun to hate his wife!" said Nichols.
"When he gave her a venereal disease, and she forgave him—he wanted
to kill her then, deep down in his unconscious. But of course the idea
couldn't enter his conscious mind—because he 'loved' her, as she
'loved' him. He'd been on that hop for years. So, when he finally had
to kill her, knowing he had to be true to his own nature and go off to
Harry's saloon for a shot of Hope, a big drunk and a week with the
tarts and bums, he first had to cook another pill of opium and grab
the beautiful pipe dream that he was killing her for love—so she
wouldn't suffer any longer from his incurable debauchery."

Hickey's delusion vanishes when he discovers that with Evelyn's
death he no longer has the desire to go off on a drunk; he is forced
to grasp at a new pipe dream—that his release from a guilt-ridden
marriage has cleansed him and removed the need for debauchery.

"How fiendishly clever the human mind is!" said Nichols. "When
one dream is punctured, when we are finally brought face to face with
ourselves or with 'reality,' the mind jumps to another pipe dream and
calls it truth—calls it facing reality!"

But Hickey's new pipe dream also vanishes when he discovers that
his friends in Harry Hope's saloon will not buy it; they are appalled
when they discover he has murdered his wife and regard it as the act
of an insane man. Hickey, forced to seize still another illusion, con-
vinces himself that his friends are right—that he is insane.

"I don't see the play as pessimistic," Nichols observed. "It's surely not
a gloomy play. O'Neill himself delighted in its laughter. He'd chuckle
over the tarts and the others—he loved them all. He didn't feel that
the fact that we live largely by illusion is sad. The important thing is
to see that we do. The quality of a man is merely the quality of his
illusions. We like illusioned people. No happy person lives on good
terms with reality. No one has even penetrated what reality is.

*   *   *

"Curiously, *The Iceman Cometh,* like any great play, reveals its
reviewers more than they reveal the play," Dudley Nichols remarked,
on the occasion of the play's successful off-Broadway revival. "All of
them complain of its length. Yet they are held by it to the end. What

is really at fault is ourselves. We have lost the faculty of sustained attention.

"I use the phrase which Gene used in telling me, years ago, why he was reluctant to have the play produced even the first time. He said we have been conditioned by radio, TV, the movies, advertising, capsule news and a nervous brevity in everything we do, to a point where we have lost the power of sustained attention, which full-bodied works of art demand.

"Unless something moves and jerks, we soon turn away from it. If it doesn't chatter or talk like a machine gun, we don't listen for long. [Walter] Winchell knows this perfectly—he adopted a style which can hold anyone's attention for fifteen minutes and make what he says sound important no matter how trivial it may be. Winchell is a master of the modern style. He is its arch-creator. Joshua Logan catches this style in the theatre; he makes things happen for the eye all the time, no matter whether the play is saying anything or not. Now, a trivial play can be all movement, but a great play cannot. . . .

"The truth is, about *The Iceman Cometh,* all kinds of things are happening all the time, but you have to listen and watch, and you hear repetition because that is the way O'Neill planned it, so that you cannot miss his meaning, and the emotions generated by his drama."

I. A PAIR OF NEGATIVES

Trying to Like O'Neill

by Eric Bentley

It would be nice to like O'Neill. He is the leading American play-wright; damn him, damn all; and damning all is a big responsibility. It is tempting to damn all the rest and make of O'Neill an exception. He *is* an exception in so many ways. He has cared less for temporary publicity than for lasting and deserved fame. When he was successful on Broadway he was not sucked in by Broadway. The others have vanity; O'Neill has self-respect. No dickering with the play doctors in Manhattan hotel rooms. He had the guts to go away and the guts to stay away. O'Neill has always had the grownup writer's concern for that continuity and development which must take place quietly and from within. In a theatre which chiefly attracts idiots and crooks he was a model of good sense and honor.

In 1946 he was raised to the American peerage: his picture was on the cover of *Time* magazine. The national playwright was interviewed by the nationalist press. It was his chance to talk rot and be liked for it. It was his chance to spout optimistic uplift and play the patriotic pundit. O'Neill said:

> I'm going on the theory that the United States, instead of being the most successful country in the world is the greatest failure . . . because it was given everything more than any other country. Through moving as rapidly as it has, it hasn't acquired any real roots. Its main idea is that everlasting game of trying to possess your own soul by the possession of something outside it too. . . .

"Trying to Like O'Neill," by Eric Bentley. From In Search of Theater *(New York, Alfred A. Knopf, Inc., 1952), pp. 331-45. Copyright © 1952, 1953 by Eric Bentley. Reprinted by permission of the publisher.*

Henry Luce possesses a good many things besides his own soul. He possesses *Life* as well as *Time,* and in the former he published an editorial complaining of the lack of inspiration to be found in the national playwright. In *The Iceman Cometh* there were no princes and heroes, only bums and drunks. This was "democratic snobbism." Henry Luce was evidently in favor of something more aristocratic (the pin-up girls in his magazine notwithstanding). Inevitably, though, what the aristocrats of *Time Inc.* objected to in O'Neill was his greatest virtue: his ability to stay close to the humbler forms of American life as he had seen them. It is natural that his claim to be a national playwright should rest chiefly on a critical and realistic attitude to American life which they reject. Like the three great Irish playwrights, O'Neill felt his "belonging" to his country so deeply that he took its errors to heart and, although admittedly he wished his plays to be universal, they all start at home; they are specifically a criticism of American life. *Marco Millions* is only the bluntest of his critical studies. Interest in the specifically American pattern of living sustains his lightest work *Ah, Wilderness!* New England patterns are integral to *Desire Under the Elms* and *Mourning Becomes Electra,* the latter being an attempt at an *Oresteia* in terms of American history, with the Civil War as an equivalent of the Trojan War. The protagonist of *The Iceman Cometh* is a product of Hoosier piety, a study much more deeply rooted in American life than Arthur Miller's of a salesman going to his death. It would be nice to like O'Neill because the Luce magazines *dis*like him—that is, because he is opposed to everything they stand for.

Last autumn, when I was invited to direct the German language *première* of *The Iceman,* along with Kurt Hirschfeld, I decided I should actually succeed in liking O'Neill. I reminded myself that he had been honored with prefaces by Joseph Wood Krutch and Lionel Trilling, that he had aroused enthusiasm in the two hardest-to-please of the New York critics, Stark Young and George Jean Nathan, and so forth. I even had a personal motive to aid and abet the pressure of pure reason. My own published strictures on O'Neill had always been taken as a display of gratuitous pugnacity, amusing or reprehensible according to my reader's viewpoint. Under a rain of dissent one begins to doubt one's opinions and to long for the joy that is not confined to heaven when a sinner repenteth. Now it is a fallacy that drama critics are strongly attached to their own opinions; actually they would far rather be congratulated on having the flexibility to change their minds. In short, I would have been glad to write something in praise of O'Neill, and I actually did lecture—and speak on the Swiss radio—as an O'Neillite. If this seems disingenuous, I can only plead that I spoke as a director, not as critic, and that it is sometimes a great relief to do so. There is something too godlike about criticism; it is a defiance of the injunction to men: Judge not that ye be not judged; it is a strain. And if it would be subhuman to give up the critical attitude for mere liking and disliking, the directorial, interpretative attitude seems a more mature and challenging alternative.

Both critic and director are aware of faults, but whereas it is the critic's job to point them out, it is the director's job to cover them up, if only by strongly bringing out a play's merits. It is not true that a director accepts a play with its faults on its head, that he must follow the playwright even into what he believes to be error. He cannot be a self-respecting interpreter without following his own taste and judgment. Thus, Hirschfeld and I thought we were doing our best by O'Neill in toning certain things down and playing others full blast. Specifically, there seemed to us to be in *The Iceman Cometh* a genuine and non-genuine element, the former, which we regarded as the core, being realistic, the latter, which we took as inessential excrescence, being expressionistic. I had seen what came of author-worshipping direction in the Theatre Guild production, where all O'Neill's faults were presented to the public with careful reverence. In order to find the essential—or at least the better—O'Neill we agreed to forego much O'Neillism.

Our designer, Teo Otto, agreed. I told him of Robert Edmond Jones's Rembrandtesque lighting and of the way in which Jones, in his sketches, tried to create the phantasmagoria of a Strindberg dream play, but Otto, though we discussed various sensational ways of setting the play—with slanting floors and Caligari corridors or what not— agreed in the end that we were taking O'Neill's story more seriously if we tried simply to underline the sheer reality, the sheer banality and ugliness, of its locale. Instead of darkness, and dim, soulfully colored lights, we used a harsh white glare, suggesting unshaded electric bulbs in a bare room. And the rooms *were* bare. On the walls Otto suggested the texture of disintegrating plaster: a dripping faucet was their only ornament. A naked girder closed the rooms in from above. And, that this real setting be seen as setting and not as reality itself, the stage was left open above the girder. While Hirschfeld and I were busy avoiding the abstractness of expressionism, Otto made sure that we did not go to the other extreme—a piddling and illusion-mongering naturalism.

To get at the core of reality in *The Iceman*—which is also its artistic, its dramatic core—you have to cut away the rotten fruit of unreality around it. More plainly stated: you have to cut. The play is far too long—not so much in asking that the audience sit there so many hours as on sheer internal grounds. The main story is meant to have suspense but we are suspended so long we forget all about it. One can cut a good many of Larry's speeches since he is forever re-phrasing a pessi-

mism which is by no means hard to understand the first time. One can
cut down the speeches of Hugo since they are both too long and too
pretentious. It is such a pretentiousness, replete with obvious and un-
imaginative symbolism, that constitutes the expressionism of the play.
Hugo is a literary conception—by Gorky out of Dostoevsky.

We cut about an hour out of the play. It wasn't always easy. Not
wishing to cut out whole characters we mutilated some till they had,
I'm afraid, no effective existence. But we didn't forget that some of the
incidental details of *The Iceman* are among O'Neill's finest achievements. Nothing emerged more triumphantly from our shortened,
crisper version than the comic elements. With a dash of good humor
O'Neill can do more than with all his grandiloquent lugubriousness.
Nothing struck my fancy more, in our production, than the little
comedy of the Boer General and the English captain. O'Neill is also
very good at a kind of homely genre painting. Harry's birthday party
with its cake and candles and the whores singing his late wife's favorite
song, "She Is the Sunshine of Paradise Alley," is extremely well done;
and no other American playwright could do it without becoming
either too sentimental or too sophisticated. We tried to build the scene
up into a great theatric image, and were assisted by a magnificent character actor as Harry (Kurt Horwitz). It is no accident that the character of Harry came out so well both in New York and Zurich: the fact
is that O'Neill can draw such a man more pointedly than he can his
higher flying creations.

I am obviously a biased judge but I think Zurich was offered a more
dramatic evening than New York. The abridging of the text did lay
bare the main story and release its suspense. We can see the action as
presumably we were meant to see it. There is Hickey, and there is
Parritt. Both are pouring out their false confessions and professions
and holding back their essential secret. Yet, inexorably, though against
their conscious will, both are seeking punishment. Their two stories
are brought together through Larry Slade whose destiny, in contrast
to his intention, is to extract the secret of both protagonists. Hickey's
secret explodes, and Larry at last gives Parritt what he wants: a death
sentence. The upshot of the whole action is that Larry is brought from
a posturing and oratorical pessimism to a real despair. Once the diffuse
speeches are trimmed and the minor characters reduced to truly minor
proportions, Larry is revealed as the center of the play, and the audience can watch the two stories being played out before him.

A systematic underlining of all that is realistic in the play did, as
we hoped it would, bring the locale—Jimmy the Priest's—to successful
theatrical realization, despite the deletion of much of O'Neill's detail.
It gave body and definition to what otherwise would have remained
insubstantial and shapeless; the comedy was sharpened, the sentiment

purified. I will not say that the production realized the idea of the play which Hirschfeld, Otto, and I entertained. In theatre there is always too much haste and bungling for that. One can only say that the actuality did not fall further short of the idea in this instance than in others.

And yet it was not a greater success with the public than the New York production, and whereas the New York critics were restrained by awe before the national playwright, the Swiss critics, when they were bored, said so. My newly won liking for O'Neill would perhaps have been unshaken by the general opinion—except that in the end I couldn't help sharing it.

I enjoyed the rehearsal period—unreservedly. I didn't have to conceal my reservations about O'Neill out of tact. They ceased to exist. They were lost in the routine, the tension, and the delight of theatre work. I don't mean to suggest that you could lose yourself thus in any script, however bad; there are scripts that bear down on a director with all the dead weight of their fatuity. But in an O'Neill script there are problems, technical and intellectual, and every one a challenge. I gladly threw myself headlong into that mad joy of the theatre in which the world and its atomic bombs recede and one's own first night seems to be the goal toward which creation strives.

The shock of the first night was the greater. It was not one of those catastrophic first nights when on all faces you can see expectancy fading into ennui or lack of expectancy freezing into a smug I Told You So. But, theatrically speaking, mild approval is little better. Theatrical art is a form of aggression. Like the internal combustion engine it proceeds by a series of explosions. Since it is in the strictest sense the most shocking of the arts, it has failed most utterly when no shock has been felt, and it has failed in a large measure when the shock is mild. *The Iceman* aroused mild interest, and I had to agree that *The Iceman* was only mildly interesting. When I read the critics, who said about my O'Neill production precisely what I as critic had said about other O'Neill productions, my period of liking O'Neill was over.

Of course there were shortcomings which could not be blamed on O'Neill. We were presenting him in German, and in addition to the normal translation problems there were two special ones: that of translating contrasting dialects and that of reproducing the tone of American, semi-gangster, hardboiled talk. There was little the translator could do about the dialects. She wisely did not lay under contribution the various regions of Germany or suggest foreign accents, and her idea of using a good deal of Berlin slang had to be modified for our Swiss public. One simply forewent many of O'Neill's effects or tried to get them by non-verbal means—and by that token one realized how much O'Neill does in the original with the various forms of the

vernacular spoken in New York. One also realizes how much he uses
the peculiarly American institution of Tough Talk, now one of the
conventions of the American stage, a lingo which the young playwright
learns, just as at one time the young poet learned Milton's poetic dic-
tion. In German there seems to be no real equivalent of this lingo because there is no equivalent of the psychology from which it springs
and to which it caters. And there is no teaching the actors how to
speak their lines in the hardboiled manner. Irony is lost, and the
dialogue loses its salt. This loss and that of dialect flavor were undoubtedly great deficiencies. But not the greatest. I saw the production
several times and, in addition to the flaws for which we of the Schau-
spielhaus were responsible, there stood out clearer each time the known,
if not notorious, faults of O'Neill. True, he is a man of the theatre
and, true, he is an eloquent writer composing, as his colleagues on
Broadway usually do not, under the hard compulsion of something he
has to say. But his gifts are mutually frustrating. His sense of theatrical
form is frustrated by an eloquence that decays into mere repetitious
garrulousness. His eloquence is frustrated by the extreme rigidity of the
theatrical mold into which it is poured—jelly in an iron jar. Iron.
Study, for example, the stage directions of *The Iceman,* and you will
see how carefully O'Neill has drawn his ground plan. There everyone
sits—a row of a dozen and a half men. And as they sit, the plot progresses; as each new stage is reached, the bell rings, and the curtain
comes down. Jelly. Within the tyrannically, mechanically rigid scenes,
there is an excessive amount of freedom. The order of speeches can be
juggled without loss, and almost any speech can be cut in half.

The eloquence might of course be regarded as clothing that is necessary to cover a much too mechanical man. Certainly, though we
gained more by abridging the play than we lost, the abridgement did
call attention rather cruelly to the excessively schematic character of
the play. Everything is contrived, *voulu,* drawn on the blackboard,
thought out beforehand, imposed on the material by the dead hand of
calculation. We had started out from the realization that the most life-
less schemata in this over-schematic play are the expressionistic ones
but we had been too sanguine in hoping to conceal or cancel them.
They are foreshadowed already in the table groupings of Act One (as
specified in O'Neill's stage directions). They hold the last act in a
death grip. Larry and Parritt are on one side shouting their duet.
Hickey is in the center singing his solo. And at the right, arranged
en bloc, is everyone else, chanting their comments in what O'Neill
himself calls a "chorus."

It would perhaps be churlish to press the point, were O'Neill's ambition in this last act not symptomatic both of his whole endeavor
as a playwright and of the endeavor of many other serious playwrights

in our time. It is the ambition to transcend realism. O'Neill spoke of it nearly thirty years ago in a note on Strindberg:

> It is only by means of some form of "super-naturalism" that we may express in the theatre what we comprehend intuitively of that self-obsession which is the particular discount we moderns have to pay for the loan of life. The old naturalism—or realism if you will (I wish to God some genius were gigantic enough to define clearly the separateness of these terms once and for all!) —no longer applies. It represents our fathers' daring aspirations towards self-recognition by holding the family kodak up to ill-nature. But to us their audacity is blague, we have taken too many snapshots of each other in every graceless position. We have endured too much from the banality of surfaces.

So far, so good. This is only a warning against that extreme and narrow form of realism generally known as naturalism. Everyone agrees. The mistake is only to talk as if it followed that one must get away from realism altogether, a mistake repeated by every poetaster who thinks he can rise above Ibsen by writing flowerily (e.g. Christopher Fry as quoted and endorsed by *Time* magazine). Wherever O'Neill tries to clarify his non-realistic theory the only thing that is clear is lack of clarity. For example:

> It was far from my idea in writing *The Great God Brown* that the background pattern of conflicting tides in the soul of man should ever overshadow and thus throw out of proportion the living drama of the recognizable human beings. . . . I meant *it* always to be mystically within and behind them, giving them a significance beyond themselves, forcing itself through them to expression in mysterious words, symbols, actions they do not themselves comprehend. And that is as clearly as I wish an audience to comprehend *it*. *It* is Mystery—the mystery any one man or woman can feel but not understand as the meaning of any event—or accident—in any life on earth. And it is this mystery which I want to realize in the theatre.

I have italicized the word *it* to underline the shift in reference that takes place. The first two times "it" is "the background pattern of conflicting tides in the soul of man." The third time "it" is just a blur, meaning nothing in particular, exemplifying rather than clearing up the mystery which O'Neill finds important. An event can be mysterious, but how can its mystery be its meaning? And how can we know that its mystery is its meaning if we do "not understand" it? And what would constitute a "realization" of such a phenomenon in the theatre?

In a letter to Thomas [sic] Hobson Quinn, O'Neill tries again. He has been seeking to be a poet, he says,

> and to see the transfiguring nobility of tragedy, in as near the Greek sense as one can grasp it, in seemingly the most ignoble, debased lives.

And just here is where I am a most confirmed mystic too, for I'm always, always trying *to interpret Life in terms of lives, never just lives in terms of characters.* I'm always acutely conscious of the Force behind (Fate, God, our biological past creating our present, whatever one calls it— Mystery certainly) and of the one eternal tragedy of Man in his glorious, self-destructive struggle *to make the Force express him instead of being, as an animal is, an infinitesimal incident in its expression.* And my profound conviction is that this is the only subject worth writing about and that it is possible—or can be—to develop [syntax?] a tragic expression in terms of transfigured modern values and symbols in the theatre which may to some degree bring home to members of a modern audience their ennobling identity with the tragic figures on the stage. Of course, this is very much of a dream, but where theatre is concerned, one must have a dream and the Greek dream in tragedy is the noblest ever!

I have italicized this time phrases where we expect O'Neill to say something, where we even think for a moment that he *has* said something. Reading them several times over, we find that we could give them a meaning—but without any assurance that it is O'Neill's. What is interpreting "Life in terms of lives" and what is "mystical" about it? What does it mean to be "expressed" by a Force—as against being an incident in "its expression"? Isn't O'Neill comforting himself with verbiage? For what connection is there—beyond the external ones of *Mourning Becomes Electra*—between his kind of drama and the Greek? How could one be ennobled by identifying oneself with any of his characters?

It is no use wanting to get away from realism (or anything else) unless you know what you want to get away *to.* Raising a dust of symbols and poeticisms is not to give artistic expression to a sense of mystery. It is merely, in O'Neill's case, to take your eye off the object. (Cf. Ibsen: "To be a poet is chiefly to see.") It seems to me that O'Neill's eye was off the object, and on Dramatic and Poetic Effects, when he composed the Hickey story. Not being clearly seen, the man is unclearly presented to the audience: O'Neill misleads them for several hours, then asks them to reach back into their memory and re-interpret all Hickey's actions and attitudes from the beginning. Is Hickey the character O'Neill needed as the man who tries to deprive the gang of their illusions? He (as it turns out) is a maniac. But if the attempt to disillude the gang is itself mad, it would have more dramatic point made by a sane idealist (as in *The Wild Duck*).

Does O'Neill find the meaning of his story by looking at the people and the events themselves or by imposing it on them? There are ideas in the play, and we have the impression that what should be the real substance of it is mere (not always deft) contrivance to illustrate the ideas. The main ideas are two: first the one we have touched on, that people may as well keep their illusions; second, that one should not hate and punish but love and forgive. The whole structure of the play is so inorganic, it is hardly to be expected that the two ideas would be organically related. The difficulty is in finding what relation they do have. In a way the truth-illusion theme is a red herring, and, as in *Cosi è (se vi pare)*, the author's real interest is in the love-hate theme. Pirandello, however, presents the red herring *as* a red herring, relates his "false" theme to this real one. O'Neill is unclear because he fails to do so. A high official of the Theatre Guild remarked: "the point is, you aren't *meant* to understand." In Pirandello this is indeed the point of the Ponza/Frola story. Pirandello *makes* the point, and in art a point has to be made before it can be said to exist. For O'Neill it is merely a point he might have made. As things are, it is his play, and not life, that is unintelligible.

The Iceman, of course, has big intentions written all over it. Most of O'Neill's plays have big intentions written all over them. He has written of

> the death of an old God and the failure of science and materialism to give any satisfying new one for the surviving primitive religious instinct to find a meaning for life in, and to comfort its fears of death with. It seems to me [he adds] anyone trying to do big work nowadays must have this subject behind all the little subjects of his plays or novels.

In other words, O'Neill's intentions as a writer are no less vast than Dostoevsky's. *The Iceman* is his version of crime and punishment. What is surprising is not that his achievements fall below Dostoevsky's but that critics—including some recent rehabilitators—have taken the will for the deed and find O'Neill's "nobler conception" of theatre enough. "Conception" is patently a euphemism for "intention" and they are applauding O'Neill for strengthening the pavement of hell. In this they are not disingenuous; their own intentions are also good; they are simply a party to a general gullibility. People believe what they are told, and in our time a million units of human energy are spent on the telling to every one that is spent on examining what is told; reason is swamped by propaganda and publicity. Hence it is that an author's professions and intentions, broadcast not only by himself but by an army of interested and even disinterested parties, determine what people think his work is. The realm of false culture thus created is not all on one level; brows here, as elsewhere, may be low or high. No brows are higher indeed than those of the upper stratum of the subintelligentsia. They spend their time seeking sublimities, works which provide the answers to the crying questions of our time, impassioned appeals for justice, daring indictments of tyranny, everything surefire. Seek and you shall find: a writer like O'Neill does not give them the optimism of an "American century" but he provides pro-

fundities galore, and technical innovations, and (as he himself says)
Mystery. Now there is a large contingent of the subintelligentsia in the
theatre world. They are seen daily at the Algonquin and nightly at
Sardi's. They don't all like O'Neill, yet his "profound" art is incon-
ceivable without them. O'Neill doesn't like *them,* but he needs them,
and could never have dedicated himself to "big work" had their voices
not been in his ears telling him he was big. The man who could not
be bribed by the Broadway tycoons was seduced by the Broadway
intelligentsia.

At one time he performed a historic function, that of helping the
American theatre to grow up. In all his plays an earnest attempt is
made to interpret life; this fact in itself places O'Neill above his pred-
ecessors in American drama and beside his colleagues in the novel and
poetry. He was a good playwright insofar as he kept within the somewhat narrow range of his own sensibility. When he stays close to a
fairly simple reality and when, by way of technique, he uses fairly simple forms of realism or fairly simple patterns of melodrama, he can
render the bite and tang of reality or, alternatively, he can startle and
stir us with his effects. If he is never quite a poet, he is occasionally
able—as we have seen in *The Iceman*—to create the striking theatric
image.

But the more he attempts, the less he succeeds. *Lazarus Laughed*
and *The Great God Brown* and *Days Without End* are inferior to
The Emperor Jones and *Anna Christie* and *Ah, Wilderness!.* O'Neill
has never learned this lesson. The idea of "big work" lured him out
into territory where his sensibility is entirely inoperative. Even his
most ardent admirers have little to say in favor of *Dynamo,* the only
play where he frontally assails the problem of "the death of an old
God and the failure of science." A hundred novelists have dealt more
subtly with hidden motives than O'Neill did in his famous essay in
psychological subtlety, *Strange Interlude,* a play which is equally inferior as a study of upper-class Americans. Then there is his desire to
re-create ancient tragedy. Though no one is more conscious than he
that America is not an Athens, the "Greek dream"—the desire to be an
Aeschylus—has been his nightmare.

The classic and notorious problem about tragedy in modern dress
has been that the characters, not being over life-size but rather below
it, excite pity without admiration and therefore without terror.
Though O'Neill has talked of an "ennobling identification" with
protagonists, he has only once tried to do anything about it: only in
Mourning Becomes Electra are the characters over life-size. Unhappily
this is not because of the size of their bones but, as it were, by inflation
with gas, cultural and psychological.

The cultural gas is the classic story. The use of classic stories has been customary for so long, and has recently come into such vogue again, that writers have forgotten their obligation to make the stories their own. They figure that the Aeschylean names will themselves establish the dignity and identity of the subject, while they —the modern adaptors—get the credit and draw the royalties. They are not necessarily conscious opportunists. They probably assume, with some psychologists and anthropologists, that archetypal patterns of myth elicit profound responses of themselves, irrespective of presentation; if this were true the poet would be unnecessary; it is a belief not to be discussed by a critic since the very act of criticism presupposes its falsity. If we ask what difference it makes that Orin and Lavinia are versions of Orestes and Electra the answer is that they thereby acquire an artificial prestige. They have become more important without any creative work on the author's part. We now associate them with the time-honored and sublime. They are inflated with cultural gas. It's like finding out that your girl friend is the daughter of a duke. If you are impressionable, you are impressed; she will seem different from now on, clad in all your illusions about nobility.

We are told that myth is useful because the audience knows the plot already and can turn its attention to the how and why. To this I would not protest that all adaptors, including O'Neill, change the mythic plots, though this is true; what I have in mind is, rather, that they do not always change them enough. Events in their works have often no organic place there, they are fossilized vestiges of the older version. We ask: why does this character do that? And the answer is: because his Greek prototype did it. In *Mourning Becomes Electra* the myth makes it hard for O'Neill to let his people have their own identity at all, yet to the extent that they do have one, it is, naturally, a modern and American identity, and this in turn makes their ancient and Greek actions seem wildly improbable. Heaven knows that murders take place today as in ancient times; but the murders in O'Neill are not given today's reality.

Instead, the characters are blown up with psychological gas. O'Neill has boasted his ignorance of Freud but such ignorance is not enough. He should be ignorant also of the watered-down Freudianism of Sardi's and the Algonquin, the Freudianism of all those who are ignorant of Freud, the Freudianism of the subintelligentsia. It is through this Freudianism, and through it alone, that O'Neill has made the effort, though a vain one, to assimilate the myth to modern life. Now what is it that your subintellectual knows about Freud? That he "put everything down to sex." Precisely; and that is what O'Neill does with the myth. Instead of reverent family feeling to unite an Orestes and an Electra we have incest. *Mourning Becomes*

Electra is all sex talk. Sex *talk*—not sex lived and embodied but sex talked of and fingered. The sex talk of the subintelligentsia. It is the only means by which some sort of eloquence and urgency gets into the play, the source of what is meant to be its poetry. The Civil War never gains the importance it might have had in this telling of the story, it is flooded out by sex. "New England," surely a cultural conception with wider reference than this, stands only, in O'Neill, for the puritanic (i.e. sexually repressive) attitude.

O'Neill is an acute case of what Lawrence called "sex in the head." Sex is almost the only idea he has—has insistently—and it is for him *only* an idea. Looking back on what I wrote about him a few years ago, I still maintain that O'Neill is no thinker. He is so little a thinker, it is dangerous for him to think. To prove this you have only to look at the fruits of his thinking; his comparatively thoughtless plays are better. For a non-thinker he thinks too much.

Almost as bad as sex in the head is tragedy in the head, for tragedy too can decline into a doctrine and dwindle into an idea. And when the thing is absent its "idea" is apt to go soft. Tragedy is hard, but the idea of tragedy ("the tragic view of life," "the tragic sense of life" etc.) is seldom evoked without nostalgic longing. And the most decadent longing is the longing for barbarism, *nostalgie de la boue,* such as is voiced by our tragedy-loving poets:

> Poetry is not a civilizer, rather the reverse, for great poetry appeals to the most primitive instincts. . . . Tragedy has been regarded, ever since Aristotle, as a moral agent, a purifier of the mind and emotions. But the story of *Medea* is about a criminal adventurer and his gun-moll; it is no more moral than the story of Frankie and Johnny; only more ferocious. And so with the yet higher summits of Greek Tragedy, the Agamemnon series and the *Oedipus Rex*; they all tell primitive horror stories, and the conventional pious sentiments of the chorus are more than balanced by the bad temper and wickedness, or folly, of the principal characters. What makes them noble is the poetry; the poetry and the beautiful shapes of the plays, and the extreme violence born of extreme passion. . . . These are stories of disaster and death, and it is not in order to purge the mind of passions but because death and disaster are exciting. People love disaster, if it does not touch them too nearly—as we run to see a burning house or a motor crash. . . .

Aristotle's view of tragedy is humane, this one—that of Robinson Jeffers—is barbaric without the innocence of barbarism; it is neobarbaric, decadent. O'Neill is too simple and earnest to go all the way with Jeffers. Puritanism and a rough-hewn honesty keep him within the realm of the human. But *Mourning Becomes Electra* does belong, so to speak, to the same world as Jeffers' remarks, a world which titillates itself with tragedy in the head. Your would-be tragedian despises realism, the problem play, liberalism, politics in general, optimism, and what not. Hence *Mourning Becomes Electra* is unrealistic, unsocial, illiberal, unpolitical, and pessimistic. What of the *Oresteia*? It celebrates the victory of law over arbitrary violence, of the community over the individual. It is optimistic, political, social and with permissible license might be called liberal and realistic as well. *O tempora, o mores!*

If one does not like O'Neill, it is not really he that one dislikes: it is our age—of which like the rest of us he is more the victim than the master.

Eugene O'Neill—Dry Ice

by Mary McCarthy

The crucial figure of O'Neill's new play is a mad hardware sales-man. Consonantly, the play itself is like some stern piece of hardware in one of those dusty old-fashioned stores into which no Pyrex dish or herb shelf or French provincial earthenware had yet penetrated, which dealt in iron-colored enamel, galvanized tin, lengths of pipe and wrenches, staples, saws, and nails, and knew nothing more sophisti-cated than the double boiler. Ugly, durable, mysteriously utilitarian, this work gives the assurance that it has been manufactured by a re-liable company; it is guaranteed to last two-and-a-half hours longer than any other play, with the exception of the uncut *Hamlet*.

The Iceman Cometh is indeed made of ice or iron; it is full of will and fanatic determination; it appears to have hardened at some ex-treme temperature of the mind. In the theatre today, it is attractive positively because of its defects. To audiences accustomed to the oily virtuosity of George Kaufman, George Abbott, Lillian Hellman, Odets, Saroyan, the return of a playwright who—to be frank—cannot write is a solemn and sentimental occasion. O'Neill belongs to that group of American authors, which includes Farrell and Dreiser, whose choice of vocation was a kind of triumphant catastrophe; none of these men possessed the slightest ear for the word, the sentence, the speech, the paragraph; all of them, however, have, so to speak, en-forced the career they decreed for themselves by a relentless policing of their beat. What they produce is hard to praise or to condemn; how is one to judge the great, logical symphony of a tone-deaf musician? Pulpy in detail, their work has nevertheless a fine solidity of structure; they drive an idea or a theme step by step to its brutal concluion with the same terrible force they have brought to bear on their profession. They are among the few contemporary American writers who know how to exhaust a subject; that is, alas, their trouble. Their logical, graceless works can find no reason for stopping, but go on and on, like elephants pacing in a zoo. In their last acts and chapters, they arrive

---

"Eugene O'Neill—Dry Ice," by Mary McCarthy. From Sights and Spectacles (*New York: Farrar, Straus, & Giroux, 1956), pp. 81-85. Copyright 1937 by Mary McCarthy. Reprinted by permission of the publisher.*

not at despair but at a strange, blank nihilism. Their heroes are all searchers; like so many non-verbal, inarticulate people, they are looking for a final Word that will explain everything. These writers are, naturally, masters of suspense.

O'Neill has neither the phenomenal memory which serves Farrell as a substitute for observation, nor the documentary habits which, for Dreiser, performed the same service. In *The Iceman Cometh*, the scene is a cheap bar somewhere in downtown New York in the year 1912; the characters are the derelict habitués of the back room—a realist's paradise, one would think. But it needs only a short walk along Third Avenue today (or the armchair method of inquiry) to solidify the suspicion that, unless drinking *moeurs* have changed in the last thirty-five years, O'Neill is an incompetent reporter. In the day and a half that elapses on the stage of the Martin Beck, none of the characters is visibly drunk, nobody has a hangover, and, with a single brief exception, nobody has the shakes; there are none of those rancorous, semi-schizoid silences, no obscurity of thought, no dark innuendoes, no flashes of hatred, there is, in short, none of the terror of drink, which, after all, in the stage that Harry Hope's customers have presumably reached, is a form of insanity. What is missing is precisely the thing that is most immediately striking and most horrifying in any human drunkard, the sense of the destruction of personality. Each of O'Neill's people is in perfect possession of the little bit of character the author has given him. The Boer is boerish, the Englishman english, the philosopher philosophizes, and the sentimental grouch who runs the establishment grouches and sentimentalizes in orderly alternation. So obedient indeed are these supposed incorrigibles to the play's thematic dictation, so well behaved in speech and in silence, that one might imagine, if one shut one's eyes, that one was attending the Christmas exercises in some respectable school ("I am Wind, I blow and blow," says little Aeolus with his bag).

And the didactic tone is, in fact, the play's natural mode. The "realistic" scene that stretches, rather Moscow Art style and friezelike, across the stage is no more than mood or *décor*. The play quickly calls itself to order, the drunkards awake and embark on an elementary study of the nature of reality and illusion. Each drunkard, it seems, has his "pipe-dream": he imagines that tomorrow he will get a job, take a walk, marry, see the anarchist millennium, go home to England or South Africa. A hardware salesman, beloved of all, who is expected to arrive for one of his periodical benders, finally does appear on the dot of the dramatist's excellent schedule; he is changed, sober, exhilarated, he has a mission to perform; he will cure Harry Hope and his customers of the illusions that are making them unhappy. In the course of the play, he obliges each of the characters to test himself.

All fail to carry out the actions projected in the pipe-dream, but self-knowledge, the recognition of failure, does not bring them the freedom the salesman promised. On the contrary, it kills whatever life was left in them; disgruntled, despairing, demoralized, they cannot even get drunk, though they are full of red-eye whiskey. Fortunately, it turns out that the salesman had attained his own state of freedom and euphoria by killing his wife; the police come for him, and Harry Hope and his clients, perceiving that he is mad, can dismiss the truths he has taught them and feel their liquor again (though this statement must be taken on faith, since here, as in the rest of the play, alcoholism does not have its customary sour breath, and the characters, like the actors who are impersonating them, seem to have been swallowing ponies of tea). As the happy derelicts carouse, one character who is without illusions, the boy who has betrayed his anarchist mother to the police, goes out and commits suicide, and another character, the philosopher, who is also capable of facing truth, indicates that he will soon join him in a plunge from the fire-escape. Life, then, consists of illusion, and if death is reality, reality is also death.

The odd thing about *The Iceman Cometh* is that this rather bony synopsis does it perfect justice; in fact, it improves it by substituting, whenever possible, the word *illusion* for the word *pipe-dream*, which recurs with a crankish and verbally impoverished tastefulness about two hundred times during the play. What shreds of naturalism cling to this work are attached to and encumber the dialogue; the language has the wooden verisimilitude, the flat, dead, echoless sound of stale slang that makes Farrell's novels and the later works of Sinclair Lewis so stilted. O'Neill here has not even the justification of sociological pedantry, which these other writers might bring forward. His intention is symbolic and philosophical, but unfortunately you cannot write a Platonic dialogue in the style of *Casey at the Bat*. O'Neill might have studied the nature of illusion through the separate relations to illusion of a group of characters (*The Three Sisters*), but his people are given but a single trait each, and they act and react, in the loss and recapture of illusion, not individually but in a body. Bare and plain, this play has the structure of an argument; its linguistic deficiencies make it maudlin. How is your wife getting along with the iceman, the characters roar, over and over again, and though death is the iceman, the joke is not appreciably refined by this symbolic treatment; rather, it is death that is coarsened.

Yet it must be said for O'Neill that he is probably the only man in the world who is still laughing at the iceman joke or pondering its implications. He is certainly the only writer who would have the courage or the lack of judgment to build a well-made play around it. This sense of one man's isolation is what, above all, gives *The Iceman*

Cometh its salient look. Though it is full of reminders of Saroyan (the barroom, the loose-witted philosophical talk, the appearance of the Redeemer at the middle table), of O'Casey (again the drunkards, and the tense, frightened young man who has betrayed the Cause), of Ibsen, Thornton Wilder, and even of Maxwell Anderson (the ripples of the Mooney and Sacco-Vanzetti cases which lap at the edges of a distant slum, and again the home-made philosophy) *The Iceman Cometh* seems nevertheless estranged from all influences and impressions. Its solitariness inside its rigid structure suggests the prison or the asylum or the sound of a man laughing in a square, empty room.

The Historical Background of
The Iceman Cometh

by John Henry Raleigh

O'Neill's finest histories [historical plays] are autobiographies as
well, and take place in the "remembered" past, in the early twentieth
century: *Ah, Wilderness!*, *The Iceman Cometh*, *A Long Day's Journey
Into Night*, *A Moon for the Misbegotten*, and *Hughie*. Even though
O'Neill never completed his consciously planned cycle of plays on
American history, he did nevertheless, albeit unconsciously, finally
leave an "American" cycle if we look at the nineteenth- and twentieth-
century American plays as an historical unit and sequence, despite the
fact that only in *Long Day's Journey Into Night* and *A Moon for the
Misbegotten* is there a carry-over of characters. The sequence would
cover exactly one century, from *A Touch of the Poet* (1828) to *Hughie*
(1928), from the era of Adams-Jackson to that of Hoover. The historical character of most of these plays is underlined by the fact that they
seldom take place in a vacuum. The Adams-Jackson presidential con-
test is as integral to the background of *A Touch of the Poet* as the
Great Depression is to *Hughie*. Even the apolitical and asocial *Long
Day's Journey* and *A Moon for the Misbegotten* remind us, if ever so
slightly, of the existence of, and the wealth of, the Standard Oil Company.
The twentieth-century plays in the historical category divide themselves into the directly autobiographical, *Long Day's Journey* and *A
Moon for the Misbegotten*, about O'Neill and his family; the obliquely
autobiographical, *Ah, Wilderness!*, based on a family the O'Neills
knew in New London; *The Iceman Cometh*, dealing with characters
O'Neill knew in his down-and-out days in New York; and *Hughie*. (I
do not know, nor does any student of O'Neill as yet, so far as I know,

"*The Historical Background of* The Iceman Cometh," *by John Henry Raleigh.
From* The Plays of Eugene O'Neill (*Carbondale, Ill.: Southern Illinois University
Press, 1965*), *pp. 66-75. Copyright © 1965 by Southern Illinois University Press.
Reprinted by permission of the publisher.*

the living sources for the characters and conceptions in the last. If such exist I suppose some day a scholar will identify them.) If sorrow envelopes *Long Day's Journey* and *A Moon for the Misbegotten* and pathos is the note of *Hughie,* it is nostalgia that envelopes *Ah, Wilderness!* and, less obviously and less inconclusively, *The Iceman Cometh.* The various tragedies, and the themes, of *The Iceman Cometh* are so bleak that as the humor of the play is almost completely overlooked, so its nostalgic elements are set aside or unremarked. Yet *The Iceman Cometh* is, in part, a companion piece for *Ah, Wilderness!,* looking back from the middle of the twentieth century at pre-World War I America and seeing it through the indulgent, but not falsifying, haze of nostalgia. Nostalgia is the only kind of sentimentality that is honest and, in the later plays, this is the only sentimentality in which O'Neill indulged.

The nostalgic element in *The Iceman Cometh* is rather complicated by the fact that, though the time of the play is 1912, the characters are practically all living in the past, in most cases a long-ago past; so that the nostalgia is really about the late nineteenth century. Larry, for example, had left "The Movement" (anarchism) eleven years before, or in 1901, but he had been in it for thirty years, which means he joined it in 1871. Harry Hope had not been out of his saloon for twenty years, or since 1892. The song sung in Acts I and II, "She's the Sunshine of Paradise Alley" (the melody of which was taken from Mascagni's *Cavalleria Rusticana*), about which Cora exclaims, "I've forgotten dat has-been tune," was composed by Walter H. Ford and John W. Bratton and became popular in 1895.[1] The Boer War, which figures so prominently in the memories and motivations of Wetjoen and Lewis, took place in 1899-1902. Hickey's story of his life—the forty-five minute monologue that forms the climax of the play—has, in great part, nineteenth-century America for its backdrop since he is about fifty and therefore must have been born around 1862. In fact about the only way that the America of 1912 gets into the play is in references to the I.W.W. and to "de Bull Moosers" mentioned in Act I by Margie and Pearl, and the bombing in which Parritt's mother was involved. But the New York that Joe, Harry, and the other New Yorkers remember and dote upon is the good old days—"Dem old days!"—richly, unashamedly corrupt, automobile-less, peopled with such giants as Richard Croker, "Big Tim" Sullivan, John L. Sullivan, and Jim Corbett, whose framed photographs are seen over the mirror behind the bar in Act III, and with Harry's termagant wife, now deceased, transformed into a loving spouse. Even the fall of Oban's father, the King of the Bucket Shops, must go back five years or so to 1907. Bucket

[1] For my information about American popular music I am relying on Sigmund Spaeth's invaluable *A History of Popular Music in America* (New York, 1948).

shops, which first came into existence after the Civil War, were sham stockbrokerages which really gambled in the stock market. Their first big heyday was from 1900 to 1907. A financial panic wiped them out in 1907, but they had their greatest, and final, resurgence from 1917 to 1929.

In other words, the days most of the New Yorkers are talking about are those of the 1890's, one of the most flourishing periods of Tammany Hall [2] when Richard Croker, the most autocratic and ruthless of the Tammany bosses and the one who dominated the organization from 1886 to 1902, had corruption organized on a hitherto unparalleled scale. "Big Tim" Sullivan, also known as "The Big Feller," was the political boss of the Sixth District of Manhattan, the East Side below Fourteenth Street, but he was such a power in Tammany itself that he was one of the real leaders of the organization as a whole, so much so that no one could be the boss of Tammany without his consent and support. The conjunction of the two prize fighters, John L. Sullivan and Jim Corbett, with the two politicians, Croker and Sullivan, was not fortuitous, for both Croker and Sullivan were known for, and got their political start with, their prowess with their fists; in the "good old days" this was how an aspiring young politician first made his mark.

By 1912, when *The Iceman Cometh* takes place, Croker had long since retired from the scene, and in that year "Big Tim" Sullivan went insane and was confined. Sullivan, whatever his sins and they were many, up to and including the direction of organized crime, was one of the most colorful and likable of the old leaders and was, in fact, the last of the important "old-style" leaders, who kept a saloon, knew everybody personally, led parades, provided Thanksgiving and Christmas dinners for the poor, had a taste for public sentiment and melo-

---

[2] The literature on Tammany Hall is considerable and tends to verge into two extremes, whitewash and diatribe; the diatribe is preponderant and rightly so. As James Bryce said about Tammany: "The phenomena of municipal democracy in the United States are the most remarkable and least laudable which the modern world has witnessed; and they present some evils which no political philosopher, however unfriendly to popular government, appears to have foreseen, evils which have scarcely showed themselves in the cities of Europe, and unlike those which were thought characteristic of the rule of the masses in ancient times" (*The American Commonwealth* [New York, 1913], II, 379). The two most comprehensive histories, both in scope and documentation, of Tammany Hall are those of Gustavus Myers, *The History of Tammany Hall* (New York, 1901; revised, 1917); and M. R. Werner, *Tammany Hall* (New York, 1928). I am relying on these two books for my facts. The most interesting "inside" document is W. R. Riordon's *Plunkitt of Tammany Hall* (New York, 1948). George Washington Plunkitt was a district leader, like Sullivan, although not nearly so powerful, who in a series of conversations explained his "philosophy of government" to a newspaper reporter, William Riordon, who first published these conversations in 1905.

drama, and so on.[3] The year 1912 also witnessed the notorious Blumenthal murder which publicly exposed New York police corruption and eventuated in the setting up of a commission, the Curran Committee of the Board of Aldermen, to investigate the police. At least one old-time New York "character," "Big Dick" Butler, thought that 1912 marked the real end of the "good old days."[4] Since 1902 the boss of Tammany had been Charles Murphy, sometimes known as "Sir Charles" or "Charles I," a closemouthed man who lived on a dignified estate on Long Island, complete with a nine-hole golf course. While in town he could be met, by those he really wanted to see, only by his summons to a luxurious suite on the second floor of Delmonico's restaurant. At the Hall he was seen by those who requested to see him. Since the décor of the establishment at Delmonico's was red, it was known as "The Scarlet Room of Mystery." With reference to Murphy's previous life as a ward leader, Gustavus Meyers remarked: "Mr. Murphy's habits as a leader at this time were in singular contrast with those of years previously when, as a district leader, he had made his hailing place a lamp post. He now used a luxurious suite of rooms at Delmonico's fashionable restaurant" (p. 355). The mayors of New York at this time, the first decade of the twentieth century, were by and large respectable. The most important change in Tammany was that some of the visitors to "The Scarlet Room of Mystery" were powerful

[3] On October 31, 1909, "Big Tim" Sullivan made his only public speech, touching on experiences and sentiments which made up the apologia of James Tyrone in Act IV of *Long Day's Journey Into Night.* It was the end of a bitter political campaign, and Tammany and Sullivan had been subjected to many charges of corruption. Miner's Theatre, which Sullivan owned, was engaged for the occasion, and to a full house, with tears running down his pink cheeks, "Big Tim" made his justificatory speech for himself and for the Tammany-type politician. It was a masterpiece of melodrama and sentiment and not without a good deal of truth. Its key passage was just like the key passage of James Tyrone's account in *Long Day's Journey* about his childhood; in fact, the two situations were identical as to the number of children involved (six), the absence of a father, and the sweet, martyr-like mother: "I was born in poverty, one of six children, four boys and two girls. The boys used to sleep in a three-quarters bed, not big enough for two, and the girls in a shakedown on the floor. Some nights there was enough to eat and some nights there wasn't. And our old mother used to sing to us at night and maybe it would be the next day before we would think she had been singing but that she had gone to bed without anything to eat.

"That's the kind of people we come from, and that is the kind of mothers that bore us down here. If we can help some boy or some father to another chance we are going to give it to them" (Werner, p. 503). It would be tempting to think that Eugene O'Neill had heard, or heard of, this speech, but he had left New York for Honduras in early October 1909.

[4] Richard J. Butler and Joseph Driscoll, *Dock Walloper* (New York, 1933): "I was one of those mourners when the crêpe-hanging reformers began getting the upper hand. The wide-open town was killed in 1912, when the Becker-Blumenthal scandal broke, . . ." (p. 112).

58   *John Henry Raleigh*

and respectable, nominally anyway, financiers and businessmen with
whom Murphy carried on business within the law. In short, the façade
of Tammany had become respectable and many of its dealings had
the odor of sanctity, because, as M. R. Werner says, Murphy taught
Tammany that "more money could be made by a legal contract than
by petty blackmail" (p. 557). Not that Tammany's connections with
vice and corruption had disappeared by 1912; to the contrary they
flourished, but in a more discreet, less open, fashion. (Police corruption had in fact actually been curtailed somewhat, in the large sense.)
Twice in *The Iceman Cometh* McGloin, who had been thrown off the
Police Force in "the good old days" for being *too* greedy, speaks long-
ingly of what is going on in the "reformed" present: "Man alive, from
what the boys tell me, there's sugar galore these days" (II). And Rocky
must pay the police to protect his two tarts, Pearl and Margie. Still, as
Larry says to Parritt in his characterization of McGloin in Act I, Mc-
Gloin's day was "back in the flush times of graft when everything
went." Then when the usual reform investigation came, McGloin was
caught red-handed and thrown off the Police Force. After describing
McGloin, Larry nods at Joe Mott and remarks that Mott had "a yesterday in the same flush period. He ran a colored gambling house."
    Through Mott's reminiscences in Act I we have a concrete vignette
of what the flush period was like, as he describes how he was permitted
to set up his gambling house. He had saved his money and had gotten
a letter to "de Big Chief" from Harry, who at that time was a minor
Tammanyite and knew the Chief. "De Big Chief" in the play is called
"Big Bill," but in reality it must have been "Big Tim" Sullivan,
whose special province was control of gambling and gambling houses
during the Croker period.[5] Of the physical size of "de Chief" there
can be no doubt, for Joe Mott dwells on it: sitting down, "big as a
freight train"; standing up, "big as two freight trains"; and with a
fist "like a ham." He roars at Joe to scare him and then gives quiet
permission to open, and, as Joe says, "I run wide open for years." For
the flush times were the years of the magic "word": no laws, docu-
ments, or formal agreements, just the personal say-so from the right
person. As McGloin puts it in Act III: "All I've got to do is see the
right ones and get them to pass the word. They will, too. They know
I was framed. And once they've passed the word, it's as good as done,
law or no law." Harry himself was once, in Larry's phrase, a "jitney
Tammany politician" whom in 1892, the year of Bessie's death, "the
boys" were going to nominate for Alderman: "It was all fixed" (I). Almost immediately though, and in characteristic *Iceman Cometh* fash-

<hr>

[5] Sullivan, Frank Farrell, the leading professional gambler of the day, and William
S. Devery, Chief of Police of New York, ran the gambling syndicate (Werner, p.
416).

ion, it is suggested that "the boys" were going to run him only because they knew they were going to lose the ward anyway. Still, Harry had once known the right people, as Joe Mott attests; and, as the general stage directions say, he still possesses friends, sufficiently so for him to evade the technicalities of present-day laws, such as the Raines Law.

The Raines Law itself is one other roadblock that stands between Harry Hope's saloon and the good old days. The implication generally, in the reminiscences of Harry, Joe Mott, Mosher, McGloin, and some of the others, is that in the 1890's Harry Hope's saloon was a relatively prosperous place; as Joe Mott says, "Dis was a first-class hangout for sports in dem days" (I). Most aspiring Tammany politicians had gotten their start not only because of their fistical prowess but by running a saloon, as had "Big Tim" Sullivan; hence the talk of running Harry for alderman of the ward, a small affair but a not at all impossible post for the well-liked owner of a "first-class hangout for sports." But in 1912 Harry Hope's saloon is decayed, seedy, the tavern of the lost, and is described by O'Neill as having become a "Raines Law hotel of the period."

The Raines Law,[6] so called after the prohibitionist Senator Raines, who was its sponsor, was passed by the New York Legislature in 1896. The intent of the law was twofold: to increase the excise tax on the sale of liquor and to cut down the number of dealers in liquor in the state of New York. To effect these two changes the law declared that in the licensing of an establishment which dispensed liquor to be consumed on the premises, there should be no distinction between the types of establishments, as there had been hitherto. Under the Raines Law, hotels, restaurants, public houses (bars in today's parlance), and ordinary beer saloons were charged the same price, a high one, for their licenses. The distinctions that were made were statewide and were made on the basis of population, that is, the higher the population of the city or town wherein the establishment was located, the higher the price of the license. Therefore the real tax increase fell on the proprietors in New York City, and the smallest proprietors there carried the heaviest burden. When in 1903, for example, seven years after the Raines Law was enacted, the taxes were increased once more, four hundred small beer saloons were wiped out. But small proprietors in Harry Hope's class, who dealt in spirits, suffered grievously too. George Washington Plunkitt was especially incensed by the Raines Law because it discriminated against the small and poorer saloonkeeper, as contrasted to the hotelkeeper. Plunkitt claimed to have known personally of a half-dozen small saloonkeepers who, unable to pay the enormous license fee and faced with the loss of their business, committed sui-

[6] See Joseph Rountree and Arthur Sherwell, *The Taxation of the Liquor Trade* (London, 1906), pp. 352 ff.

cide. He had heard of others: "Every time there is an increase of the fee, there is an increase in the suicide record of the city" (Riordon, pp. 113-14). Whether this assertion is true cannot be proved, but certainly the enactment of the Raines Law in 1896, and its further implementation in 1903, must have seriously contributed to the decay of Harry Hope's saloon.

The Raines Law had two side effects that were not anticipated in the original legislation and that play some role in *The Iceman Cometh*. There was written into the statute a Blue Law aimed expressly at the saloons, to the effect that only hotels could serve liquor after hours and on Sundays, the times at which the saloons did some of their best business. Accordingly, every saloon that could manage to do so immediately turned itself into a "hotel restaurant," by renting rooms upstairs and by putting on the tables, in O'Neill's words, "a property sandwich . . . an old desiccated ruin of dust-laden bread and mumified ham or cheese." The most profitable thing to do with the rooms usually was to rent them out for sexual intercourse, the result being that many of the saloons became, in effect, brothels (Werner, p. 405). Now Harry Hope is still holding up his head in two respects: first, he still has enough connections at the Hall to dispense with putting out the property food on the tables (*"except during the fleeting alarms of reform agitation"*), and, second, although he has tarts rooming at his establishment, they do not carry on their trade there. As Harry says in Act I, "Never thought I'd see the day when Harry Hope's would have tarts rooming in it. What'd Bessie think? But I don't let 'em use my rooms for business." Still, he and his kind have fallen on evil times, and most of the New York characters in the play, while they lament and glorify their individual mistakes and past, are also paying a collective obsequy to the "good old days," the 1890's, when giants walked the earth, when corruption was direct, open, and simple, when "de Chief," whoever he was, was tangible and approachable, and when they were respectable "middle-class" (neither powers nor riffraff) members of the Tammany organization. The circus, and its ways, have provided the same frame of memory for Mosher.

This collective nostalgia blends into the private nostalgia of each character, New Yorker or not. It is, I think, an oversimplification to say that all these characters are special cases of preoccupation with the past because they are failures and down-and-outers; rather they represent, each in his own way, the real vagaries of the human memory, which must both simplify and glorify, if ever so slightly in a more happy and healthy climate than that of *The Iceman Cometh*, the past. It is not that all men have been fired from their jobs as drunks and thieves, as have some of the characters in *The Iceman*, but all men have done things they would like to forget and they all have at least some happy memories, which they would like to be even happier, and simpler, and to have bulked larger, in time and importance, than they actually had done in reality. It is by use of an artistically, artificially shaped past that man defends himself against the threatening present and the ominous future. A man is only genuinely lost when the past contains something mortal and deadly, like Hickey's murder of his wife and Parritt's betrayal of his mother. Almost anything else memory can take care of.

Music is, of course, the great evocator of memory, and especially in middle-class and lower-class America is popular music expressive of certain sentimental certainties that the memory would like to believe in and re-embrace, hastening back over the years to simpler and happier times and occasions. This is why popular songs play a role in *The Iceman Cometh* and even more of a role in *Ah, Wilderness!*

Popular songs gravitate between the bawdy and the sentimental; thus the two songs sung in *The Iceman Cometh* are Oban's "Sailor Lad" ditty (bawdy) and "She's the Sunshine of Paradise Alley" (sentimental). The choruses of songs dealt out to the various characters at the end, with Hickey gone, the "booze" working again, the present and future banished, were carefully chosen to perform two nostalgic functions: first, to awaken memories in the minds of the older people in the audience of the 1940's who saw the play performed for the first time and who, like the playwright, had memories of pre-World War I America, and, second, to invoke nostalgia in the minds of the characters in the play, whose memories extend back into the nineteenth century.

Although O'Neill chose his songs with extreme care for their historical date, he did commit one anachronism, a perfectly understandable one. This occurs in the musical medley at the end when Chuck is given "The Curse of an Aching Heart." Actually this song, by Henry Fink and Al Piantadosti, was not published until 1913 and could thus not have been known by people in 1912. However, the song itself was a purposeful anachronism and is made up of, in Sigmund Spaeth's phrase, "the maudlin absurdities" of the 1890's. Thus for the characters in the play it does invoke nostalgia. All the other songs sung at the end fall into one of two basic categories: either they are songs that were popular around 1912, or they are songs from the past.

"A Wee Dock and Doris," Jimmy Tomorrow's song, was published by Harry Lauder and Gerald Grafton in 1911; "Everybody's Doing It," appropriately given to Pearl and Margie, was published by Irving Berlin in 1911; "The Oceana Roll," Cora's, was done by Roger Lewis and Lucien Denni in 1911; and Rocky's "You Beautiful Doll" was perpetrated in 1911 by A. Seymour Brown and Nat Ayer. These songs, presumably, would be remembered by many of O'Neill's audience.

All the other songs, however, like "She's the Sunshine of Paradise Alley," are nostalgia-invokers for the members of the cast. Wetjoen's "Waiting at the Church" (also sung in *Ah, Wilderness!*) by Fred Leigh and Henry E. Pether, was vintage 1906; Joe Mott's "All I Got Was Sympathy" (actually the song was entitled "Sympathy"; O'Neill is using the first line of the lyrics) was put together by Kendis and Pauley in 1905; "Tammany," sung, appropriately, by McGloin, was an affectionate but lively satire on Tammany politics concocted by Gus Edwards and Vincent P. Bryan in 1905.

"Tammany" in particular, and the circumstances under which it was written illustrate most concretely what Harry Hope, Joe Mott, McGloin, and the rest mean by New York's "good old days," the time when they were part of a political corruption which was not only open, and cheerfully so, but had such a sense of humor about itself as to make it almost endearing. According to a tradition run down by Sigmund Spaeth, "Tammany" was composed under the following circumstances (whether this story is true or not, it should be): Edwards and Bryan were invited to entertain the members of New York's Democratic Club at a smoker. They had planned to introduce their new song, "In My Merry Oldsmobile," the best of many of the transportation songs of the day. But when they arrived at the smoker, the orchestra was playing a medley of the Indian songs that were so popular at the time, and so they decided, on the spot, to compose a burlesque of this type of music which would also be a political satire on Tammany, whose name was Indian in origin. The two retired to a room and worked out the chorus and two verses, with Edwards putting down the notes as fast as Bryan could write the words. In the lyrics there are references to *Hiawatha* and *Navaho*, all building up to "Big Chief Tammany." They tried out this song first on a small group of important Tammanyites, including Charlie Murphy and "Big Tim" Sullivan. With their approval, Edwards and Bryan then presented it to the whole group. It was a great and immediate success and later became the official anthem of the Tammany Society (Spaeth, pp. 347-48).

After these songs, however, we are back in the nineteenth century: Ed Mosher's "Break the News to Mother," by Charles K. Harris, was a Spanish-American War song, vintage 1897; Harry Hope's "She's the Sunshine of Paradise Alley" (1895); Oban's "Sailor Lad" ditty (the sea) is an immemorial folk song, as is Captain Lewis' "The Old Kent Road" (the land); and, of course, with Hugo's "Carmagnole" we are back to the French Revolution. As Hickey and Parritt go to their deaths, all of the other happy sinners, Larry excepted, are sinking gratefully back into nostalgia, alcoholic and tuneful.

Hugo of *The Iceman Cometh*: Realism and O'Neill

by Doris M. Alexander

Because of its obvious semantic sloppiness, the term *realism* is used with caution by critics. Usually they find safety by implying or stating their definition of *realism* when they use it. Yet such is the treachery of the concept, that a critic may be betrayed by his own definition; a critic may sincerely damn as unrealistic a work that fulfills in all respects his own definition of *realism*. Trapped in this way, by his own terminology, is the critic who describes Hugo Kalmar of *The Iceman Cometh* as "unrealistic," "literary."

In his "Trying to Like O'Neill," Eric Bentley finds the chief weakness of *The Iceman Cometh,* and of most later O'Neill plays, in the author's "ambition to transcend realism." According to Bentley, O'Neill "was a good playwright insofar as he kept within the somewhat narrow range of his own sensibility." O'Neill is artistically safe "when he stays close to a fairly simple reality and when, by way of technique, he uses fairly simple forms of realism." But when he tries to express ideas, O'Neill is, according to Bentley, lost. "He is so little a thinker, it is dangerous for him to think." This thesis, Bentley applies to *The Iceman Cometh,* finding in the play "a genuine and a non-genuine element, the former, which we regarded as the core, being realistic, the latter, which we took as inessential excrescence, being expressionistic." For this reason, Bentley finds it necessary "to cut away the rotten fruit of unreality" around the play. The one concrete instance he gives of this "rotten fruit" is the characterization of Hugo:

> One can cut down the speeches of Hugo since they are both too long and too pretentious. It is such a pretentiousness, replete with obvious and unimaginative symbolism, that constitutes the expressionism of the play. Hugo is a literary conception—by Gorky out of Dostoevsky.[1]

"Hugo of The Iceman Cometh: *Realism and O'Neill," by Doris M. Alexander. From* American Quarterly, *V (Winter, 1953), 357-66. Copyright © 1953 by* American Quarterly. *Reprinted by permission of the author and publisher.*

[1] Eric Bentley, "Trying to Like O'Neill," *Kenyon Review,* XIV, Summer 1952, pp. 476-92, and pp. 483, 488, 491, 478, 479.

When Bentley damns Hugo categorically as "a literary conception," he has either forgotten, never known, or never believed O'Neill's own statement that all the characters of *The Iceman Cometh* are people he knew personally. In the *New York Times,* October 6, 1946, Karl Schriftgriesser reported O'Neill's comment during an interview on the characters of *The Iceman Cometh:*

> "I knew 'em all," he said. "I've known 'em all for years." His voice dropped gropingly into his remembrance of things past. "All these people I have written about, I once knew."

Critics who attacked the play at the time of its Broadway production could not forget O'Neill's statement, and so they had to attack O'Neill, not for trying to "transcend realism," but rather for being unable to give an accurate representation of the reality he was offering. Take, for example, Wolcott Gibbs' criticism of *The Iceman Cometh* in the October 19, 1946, issue of the *New Yorker:*

> As several critics have pointed out, the locale of the play and the proto-types of the bums who appear in it have been taken from the author's own past. The assumption, however, that he has exactly recaptured the sound of their speech may be open to question, and it is my opinion that, while Mr. O'Neill is a superb reporter of behavior and even of processes of thought, the language he uses to convey them is actually non-realistic, being of the conventional dese-dem-dose school of dialect which a certain kind of abstracted literary intelligence, from Richard Harding Davis to Thomas Wolfe, has somewhat arbitrarily decided is the language of the lower depths. It is odd but nevertheless a fact that a writer can often understand perfectly what is being said around him without really hearing the accent of the voice or the structure of the sentence, and I'm afraid that this is particularly true of Mr. O'Neill.[2]

Of course, this criticism is aimed at all the characters, not specifically at Hugo, but that Gibbs finds Hugo particularly unconvincing appears earlier in his article where he points out that in Hugo's characterization "all that appears on the stage is a sort of irrelevant, comic-supplement bomb-thrower." [3]

In order to test the accuracy of Bentley's idea that Hugo is totally a "literary conception" or Gibbs' idea that though Hugo derives ultimately from life he has been distorted by an "abstracted literary intelligence," we would have to know definitely first whether Hugo was modeled on a living person, and second, what that living person was actually like. Fortunately, we can establish these facts with a fair amount of certainty. O'Neill's own statement that he knew all of the characters in *The Iceman Cometh* gives us our clue. If so colorful a

---

[2] Wolcott Gibbs, "The Theatre," *New Yorker* (October 19, 1946), pp. 56-57.
[3] *Ibid.,* p. 56.

character as Hugo actually existed in a literary circle like the one at Provincetown, he might appear in the memoirs of one of the group. This is exactly the case. In Mabel Dodge Luhan's *Movers and Shakers* and in Hutchins Hapgood's *A Victorian in the Modern World* are references to an extraordinary gentleman who appears to be, without a doubt, the model for O'Neill's Hugo in *The Iceman Cometh.*

Among the Provincetown group was an anarchist named Hippolyte Havel. Mabel Dodge Luhan describes him as "a Russian nihilist with a broad, low, intelligent brow, and long, black hair; he was very small, and very obscene in his talk." [4] This definition resembles, as far as it goes, O'Neill's description of Hugo Kalmar.

> Hugo is a small man in his late fifties. He has a head much too big for his body, a high forehead, crinkly long black hair streaked with gray, a square face with a pug nose, a walrus mustache, black eyes which peer near-sightedly from behind thick-lensed spectacles, tiny hands and feet. . . . There is a foreign atmosphere about him, the stamp of an alien radical, a strong resemblance to the type Anarchist as portrayed, bomb in hand, in newspaper cartoons.[5]

This description fits Mabel Dodge Luhan's, but there are not enough points of resemblance to make an absolute identification. We do not have to rely on Mabel Dodge Luhan's meager description alone, however, for in Hutchins Hapgood's *A Victorian in the Modern World* at one side of a photograph labeled "Group in Provincetown about 1916" sits Hippolyte Havel himself, and so we can compare both O'Neill's description and Mabel Dodge Luhan's with a photographic likeness of the original. From the picture it becomes clear at once that O'Neill's description of Hugo Kalmar is a better sketch of Hippolyte Havel than is Mabel Dodge Luhan's description of Havel himself. In the photograph Hippolyte's long black hair appears "crinkly," for it stands out around his head like a halo, and it is clearly streaked with gray, a detail that Mabel Dodge Luhan does not include in her description.[6] Also Mrs. Luhan's description of his "broad, low, intelligent brow" is actually, although accurate, misleading, for a "low brow" is usually associated with a low forehead, whereas the picture of Hippolyte Havel shows a positively astonishing height and breadth of forehead, so that the face appears to be pinched together at the

[4] Mabel Dodge Luhan, *Movers and Shakers,* vol. 3 of *Intimate Memories* (New York: Harcourt, Brace, 1936), p. 48. Hutchins Hapgood, who knew Hippolyte Havel better, reports: "One of Hippolyte's parents was a gypsy; and I think most of his blood was of that part of Austria called Bohemia. . . ." Hutchins Hapgood, *A Victorian in the Modern World* (New York: Harcourt, Brace, 1939), p. 198.

[5] Eugene O'Neill, *The Iceman Cometh* (New York: Random House, 1946), p. 4.

[6] Possibly Havel's hair was not as noticeably gray in 1913, when Mabel Dodge Luhan knew him, as in 1916.

bottom. The picture also confirms O'Neill's details of the square face, the pug nose, the walrus mustache, and the spectacles, which, in the photograph, are horn rimmed and very prominent.[7] The only aspect of O'Neill's description not borne out by the picture is his account of Hugo's clothing: "He is dressed in threadbare black clothes and his white shirt is frayed at collar and cuffs, but everything about him is fastidiously clean. Even his flowing Windsor tie is neatly tied." [8] We might believe that here at least O'Neill is exaggerating his original, were it not for Hapgood's description of Havel's customary attire for a weekend in Greenwich Village: "a stick, conventional black clothes, a flowing black tie, and even spats with his patent leather shoes." [9] Altogether, there are too many similarities between Hugo Kalmar and Hippolyte Havel for their resemblance to be merely a coincidence.

Nor are these similarities limited to appearance. The central facts of Hugo's life exactly parallel the main points of Hippolyte Havel's. First, in order to qualify as a member of Harry Hope's menage, Hugo is, of course, both impecunious and alcoholic. So was his original Hippolyte Havel. According to Hapgood: "Hippolyte was a determined drinker. To drink much and often was a part of his code of honor. It was limited only by his pocketbook which was usually empty, and the fact that although he had many friends, he couldn't always count on their treating him." [10] Hugo, like Hippolyte, depends on the benevolence of his friends, and O'Neill makes one of the staples of his conversation the remark: "Don't be a fool! Loan me a dollar! Buy me a trink!" [11] Apparently, even the amount of Hugo's request is patterned after his original, for Hapgood points out that Hippolyte frequently "would ask me for a dollar," and tells how once when he met Hippolyte on a Fifth Avenue bus, "he characteristically asked me for a dollar, which I dutifully handed over to him." [12] Even the more spectacular facts of Hugo's background are identical with Hippolyte's. O'Neill describes Hugo as a "one-time editor of Anarchist periodicals." [13] Hapgood tells how, when they met, Havel "was the editor of the *Arbeiterzeitung,* an Anarchist newspaper in Chicago." [14] More-

[7] O'Neill's description is also substantiated by Hutchins Hapgood's description of Havel: "He was a short, rather stocky, excitable man, with a very small nose, accentuating a high and imaginative forehead, a rather weak and sensitive chin—with a shock of black disorderly hair crowning the whole. He was in a perpetual state of vituperative excitement." Hapgood, p. 198.
[8] O'Neill, p. 4.
[9] Hapgood, p. 328.
[10] *Ibid.*
[11] O'Neill, p. 34. See also pp. 11, 104, 249.
[12] Hapgood, p. 330.
[13] O'Neill, p. v.
[14] Hapgood, p. 198.

over, even Hugo's prison experience accords with Hippolyte's. In *The Iceman Cometh* we learn from Parritt that Hugo "had the guts to serve ten years in the can in his own country and get his eyes ruined in solitary." [15] Hapgood's description of Hippolyte Havel's background is similar, although far more colorful:

> Before coming to America, Hippolyte had been sentenced to prison in an insane asylum; and, as he put it, might have been there permanently, as in that way his sentence could be indefinitely prolonged, had it not been for the visit of Krafft-Ebing, the noted psychiatrist, to the institution. After a talk with Hippolyte, Krafft-Ebing told the authorities that Hippolyte should be sent back to prison, as he was entirely sane. The great psychiatrist showed himself superior to the ordinary citizens, who, judging from Hippolyte's words and manner, might be excused for thinking him somewhere unbalanced. But anyone who knew him well, would know that he was not only sane, but much shrewder in practical things than he would ever admit. In some way he managed to escape from prison and got safe to London, where he met Emma Goldman, and with her or through her came to America and was associated with her for many years in her journalistic and oratorical propaganda.[16]

Hugo Kalmar, like his prototype Hippolyte Havel, has been an Anarchist editor, has been imprisoned in his own country, and, finally, has been and is "a determined drinker."

O'Neill has certainly been accurate in reproducing Havel's physical appearance and the main outlines of his life. But how are we to judge his accuracy in reproducing Havel's personality? Hutchins Hapgood gives us the outstanding features of Havel's personality in the following account:

> Then another character of the village whom Christine rendered with felicity was Hippolyte Havel, the wild little man about whom I have had much to say, who was always strenuously inveighing against the damn bourgeois. Although he was dark and Christine was blonde, yet, when Christine was imitating Hippolyte, the portrait was so good that Christine almost looked dark. This portrait must have been extraordinarily good because I couldn't detect any satire in it. It didn't seem to convey a criticism, perhaps because Hippolyte himself conveyed his own criticism by his actual appearance on the scene of life. This remark of mine about Hippolyte would be entirely inadequate were it not for what I have already written or shall write about him. Mean, vindictive, or jealous as Hippolyte often was, and irrationally condemnatory of almost all the world, there was in him something exquisitely sensitive, fine, and at times highly amusing in a sympathetic sense.[17]

[15] O'Neill, p. 34.
[16] Hapgood, p. 199.
[17] Hapgood, p. 426.

This description of a "wild little man" who inveighs against the "damn bourgeois" and "all the world" for that matter, who alternates between meanness, vindictiveness, and being highly amusing, seems a pretty close description of O'Neill's little anarchist, Hugo Kalmar, of *The Iceman Cometh*. Hugo's first speech reveals the essentials of his character and conversation.

> (*Raises his head and peers at* ROCKY *blearily through his thick spectacles—in a guttural declamatory tone*) Capitalist swine! Bourgeois stool pigeons! Have the slaves no right to sleep even? (*Then he grins at* ROCKY *and his manner changes to a giggling, wheedling playfulness, as though he were talking to a child*) Hello, leedle Rocky! Leedle monkey face! Vere is your leedle slave girls? (*With an abrupt change to a bullying tone*) Don't be a fool! Loan me a dollar! Damned bourgeois Wop! The great Malatesta is my good friend! Buy me a trink! [18]

Of course, there is no indication in this speech of what Hapgood refers to as "something exquisitely sensitive, fine" in Havel. But in later speeches of Hugo, O'Neill presents some sensitivity in his character, particularly in Hugo's comment on Harry deprived of his pipe dream. "Vhat's matter, Harry? You look funny. You look dead. Vhat's happened?" [19]

However, even if we have demonstrated that O'Neill conveyed accurately the substance of Havel's conversation, there is still the possibility that Gibbs is correct, and O'Neill has been unable to catch "the accent of the voice or the structure of the sentence." But even this can be checked, for Mabel Dodge Luhan has given us a specimen of Hippolyte Havel's actual conversation, which shows, by the way, how universal was his condemnation of the world as "bourgeois." She reports Havel's reactions to a conversation by Emma Goldman and Big Bill Haywood on the philosophy of the Industrial Workers of the World, and of socialism.

> "They talk like goddam bourgeois," suddenly cried Hippolyte Havel in a high, peevish voice, glaring around through the thick lenses of his spectacles.
> "My little sister!" he exclaimed to me later that evening, in his sweet whining voice. "My little goddam bourgeois capitalist sister!" And tears ran over his spectacles.[20]

Except that O'Neill is careful to represent Havel's accent, and Mabel Dodge Luhan does not attempt to, this actual specimen of Hippolyte Havel's conversation might be inserted as part of Hugo Kalmar's dialogue in *The Iceman Cometh* without any alteration but the name

[18] O'Neill, p. 11.
[19] O'Neill, p. 201.
[20] Luhan, p. 90.

of the speaker. Unless we assume that Mabel Dodge Luhan was suffer-ing from the same kind of literary astigmatism as was Eugene O'Neill, and hence both have missed the flavor of Hippolyte Havel's speech, we reach the inevitable conclusion that O'Neill has done a very accu-rate job of reporting the flavor, the style, of his original. Altogether, it is difficult to escape the conclusion that in the character of Hugo Kalmar, Eugene O'Neill has reproduced most accurately in literature a character he knew in life.[21]

What then of Eric Bentley's and Wolcott Gibbs' condemnation of Hugo as "literary," the product of an "abstracted literary intelligence"? First, what is their definition of the realism they think Hugo lacks? Bentley's definition can be gathered only by implication, but from his statement that O'Neill "was a good playwright insofar as he kept within the somewhat narrow range of his own sensibility," Bentley's realism seems to consist of a fairly photographic reproduction of life. When describing his stage set for the Berlin production of *The Iceman Cometh,* Bentley says, "we tried simply to underline the sheer reality, the sheer banality and ugliness, of its locale." Here banality and ugliness stand in apposition to reality, again suggesting a photo-graphic approach. Later Bentley points out that he didn't go "to the other extreme—a piddling and illusion-mongering naturalism." Also, when he analyzes O'Neill's note on Strindberg, Bentley comments: "So far, so good. This is only a warning against that extreme and narrow form of realism generally known as naturalism. Everyone agrees. The mistake is only to talk as if it followed that one must get away from realism altogether. . . ."[22] Bentley seems to make a quantitative dis-tinction between realism and naturalism, with naturalism simply in-cluding more details in its photograph. Whatever he holds realism to be, Bentley thinks it is endangered by philosophy, by selection on the basis of ideas. So it seems to be a fairly literal kind of reproduction of life. Gibbs' concept of realism seems very similar, since he defines the non-realism of O'Neill's dialogue as a failure to hear "the accent of the voice or the structure of the sentence" of the people he is reproducing in literature. So both critics base their idea of realism on a close repro-duction of life, and then proceed to damn as unrealistic a character who has been modeled with the utmost exactitude on a living person.

What is wrong: the critics, their terminology, or their understand-ing of their terminology? Perhaps the difficulty lies in the use of an

---

[21] It is impossible that O'Neill did not know Havel, for they were at the same place, Provincetown, at the same time, with the same friends. For instance, Hap-good met Terry Carlin, O'Neill's lifelong friend, at the anarchist ball at which he met Hippolyte Havel. Hapgood, pp. 198-99. Harry Weinberger, who appears in the Provincetown photograph with Havel, was O'Neill's lawyer and friend for many years.

[22] Bentley, p. 484.

inexact concept as an instrument of criticism. Certainly Bentley and
Gibbs cannot be blamed for finding Hugo Kalmar somewhat fantastic, just as they couldn't be blamed for finding his prototype Hippolyte Havel somewhat fantastic if they happened to meet him. The
fault is not in the judgment, but in the theory of causation. Hugo
Kalmar is fantastic not because O'Neill, bedeviled by ideas, was unable to reproduce life, but rather because O'Neill chose to reproduce
a variety of life that is inherently grotesque. What Bentley is really
objecting to in Hugo is not his lack of closeness to life, but rather
his lack of closeness to typical life. As Hutchins Hapgood observed,
Christine could not satirize Hippolyte Havel "because Hippolyte
Havel conveyed his own criticism by his actual appearance on the
scene of life." In other words, Havel's eccentricities could not be exaggerated into satire, for they were already so exaggerated that he
was a living satire. Hippolyte Havel was neither a typical human
being nor a typical anarchist. A literary reproduction of him, were
it ever so accurate, could not be more than he was himself, an eccen-
tric, a caricature. O'Neill's representation is certainly accurate. Thus
only if we assume that realism is reproduction of the typical, can we
attack Hugo for lacking it.

   Why did O'Neill choose to reproduce an atypical character like
Hippolyte Havel? Undoubtedly the same principle operated in the
selection of Hippolyte Havel as operated in the selection of all the
other characters in *The Iceman Cometh,* for all the characters are
variations on a single theme. All the characters are illustrative of a
single principle. Each must cling to a pipe dream, to a patently false
illusion, to keep from facing his own hopeless inadequacy and his
submerged hostilities toward his fellow men.[23] Which came first for
O'Neill, the principle or the characters? Karl Schriftgriesser, in his
New York Times interview with O'Neill, reported that the idea for
The Iceman Cometh came suddenly to O'Neill and that because he
knew all the characters so well, there "was not so much hard work
as if I had had to dig them out." From this statement I infer that
O'Neill's idea for *The Iceman Cometh* came from thinking of the
people like Hippolyte Havel he had known, and hence, once he had
the idea for the play, he had the characters too. Most likely O'Neill
did not alter the characters to conform to the idea, but rather saw
the idea in the characters as they were. For instance, the character
of Jimmy Tomorrow, complete with his illusion, had already appeared
in one of O'Neill's earliest plays *The Moon of the Caribbees.* In that
play he appears as the sentimental Smitty. Both as Jimmy Tomorrow

[23] For a full and very fine analysis of *The Iceman Cometh's* ideology, see Helen
Muchnic, "Circe's Swine: Plays by Gorky and O'Neill," *Comp. Lit.,* III (Spring
1951), pp. 119-28.

and as Smitty, his pipe dream consists of the illusion that he is an alcoholic because the woman he loved left him. In *The Moon of the Caribbees,* Smitty's illusion is exposed by the Donkeyman: "An' she said she threw you over 'cause you was drunk; an' you said you was drunk 'cause she threw you over." [24] In *The Iceman Cometh,* Jimmy Tomorrow, under the influence of Hickey, confesses: "And it was absurd of me to excuse my drunkenness by pretending it was my wife's adultery that ruined my life. As Hickey guessed, I was a drunkard before that. Long before." [25] Smitty needed no basic alteration to become Jimmy Tomorrow of *The Iceman Cometh,* and most likely all of the characters of *The Iceman Cometh* were as naturally illustrative of the idea of the play.

If it is correct to assume that all the characters of *The Iceman Cometh,* like Hippolyte Havel, are faithful reproductions of actual people who by their very nature are illustrative of the idea of the play, what conclusions may be drawn on the value of the play itself? First, perhaps the greatest value of the play lies in all the, to use Hugo's expression, "nice, leedle, funny monkey faces" in it. O'Neill told Barrett Clark that *The Iceman Cometh* is one of the two plays that have given him the greatest satisfaction of any he has ever done.[26] Probably his satisfaction lay in the vivid re-creation of a group of broken, but strangely lovable, people he had known. In the characters also lies, perhaps, the satisfaction of any who read or see the play. Whatever enduring value *The Iceman Cometh* holds consists, probably, not in its dramatic or ideological qualities, but in its fine character sketches of a group of fascinating lost souls.

[24] Eugene O'Neill, *The Plays of Eugene O'Neill,* 3 vols. (New York: Random House, 1941), I, 467.
[25] O'Neill, *The Iceman Cometh,* p. 229.
[26] Barrett H. Clark, *Eugene O'Neill: The Man and His Plays* (New York: Dover, 1947), p. 147.

III THE MEANING OF *The Iceman Cometh*

The Iceman Cometh: A Study in Technique

by Sophus Winther

O'Neill's latest play *The Iceman Cometh,* is his most symbolic, although it uses none of the direct symbolism of such plays as the *Great God Brown* and *Lazarus Laughed.* Anyone familiar with O'Neill's work in its entirety will recall the intricate way in which life and death, hope and fear, the dream and the reality are woven into the core of each central theme. In no other play are these symbols brought so closely together or so perfectly conceived as in *The Iceman Cometh.* In the words of Larry, one of the characters in *The Iceman Cometh,* the "worst is best here, and East is West, and tomorrow is yesterday." Later Larry gives a more comprehensive statement of the extent to which life's paradoxes are reduced to unity with all conflicts reconciled into complete nothingness.

> Honor or dishonor, faith or treachery are nothing to me but the opposites of the same stupidity which is ruler and king of life, and in the end they rot into dust in the same grave. All things are the same meaningless joke to me, for they grin at me from the one skull of death.

The recognition of the paradox[1] treated not as a clever device for satire, but as a serious instrument of tragedy is the key to the art as well as to the meaning of the play. In no other play has O'Neill combined his technical skill so completely with a searching analysis of life. No separation of thought from technique will reveal the meaning of the play. The paradox reigns supreme: the dream is the true reality, reality is a dream, hope leads to despair, despair breeds hope; the Cause, Movement, Crusade, all lead to Harry Hope's hotel, "a cheap ginmill" of the "last resort variety." The paradox brings that close juxtaposition of opposites which in time reduces all opposites to a oneness. The problem is to define clearly all operating forces in the tragedy, to identify them as irreconcilable opposites and then,

"The Iceman Cometh: *A Study in Technique,*" *by Sophus Winther. From* Arizona Quarterly, *III (Winter, 1947), 293-300. Copyright © 1946 by* Arizona Quarterly. *Reprinted by permission of the author and publisher.*

[1] See Cleanth Brooks on paradox, *The Well Wrought Urn.*

through the introduction of the proper catalyst, slowly melt them into one.

This is the common practice in great tragedy. It must test man not in the middle course of life, nor by the ordinary burdens that are a part of everyday experience. Tragedy must push man to the verge of his ultimate endurance until he stands on the bank and shoal of time, until he cries out "Let us anatomize Regan to see if there be any cause in nature that makes these hard hearts." The quality of man, like the tensile strength of steel, is measured at the breaking point. The outward contradictions provide the action which leads to the reconciliation of the paradox, an inward unity which is the tragic end.

O'Neill brings before his readers a group of characters who at the first casual glance have lost every shred of humanity. They seem to have passed the breaking point, to have reached the place of slow but inevitable decay. O'Neill compares them to dogs, turkeys, horses, monkeys; they are remnants of men, scarecrows who have in some strange manner cheated the undertaker. For them there is nothing left except pipe dreams nourished and kept alive by rotgut whisky. Before the slightest breath of the outside world they tremble and shake like an old dog in his sleep. They are utterly broken. They are dead shadows of human beings, but the paradox is that they are all this, while at the same time they are symbols of all that is meaningful in the life of man. There are among them some whose history is not revealed fully. The reason for the pimps and whores is not explained. Perhaps they need no explanation, being the normal product of a world that has brought Oban, Larry, Jimmy Tomorrow, Hugo, and Harry Hope to the brink of the ultimate Slough of Despond.

Each in his own way was destroyed by his faith in the Cause, The Big Movement, the Ideal of what man should be. Willie Oban has made his final visit to the hockshop. His few pieces of clothing look as though they were made "of an inferior grade of dirty blotting paper." His bare feet show through his ragged shoes. His face continually twitches, his eyelids blink as though the light were too strong for them. Larry is a disinterested observer. He has taken "a seat in the grandstand of philosophic detachment" from which he expects to fall asleep "observing the cannibals do their death dance." His favorite quotation is from Heine:

> Lo, sleep is good, better is death; in sooth
> The best of all were never to be born.

Hugo is neat and clean, but in some ways the most utterly desolate of them all. His one desire is enough booze to keep him asleep, his one theme, "The days grow hot, O Babylon! 'Tis cool beneath thy willow trees!"

Harry Hope, owner of the hotel which provides the setting, has not left the place for twenty years. He would seem to be the most useless of men, the most completely detached from anything that is meaningful to the normal world of men.

And so are they all upon first sight, as useless, degenerate, and physically and morally ragged as human beings could possibly be. They hang on the shadowy threads of life like spiders clinging to a hopelessly ruined and tangled web. They are sustained by a poisonous brew that should have turned them over to the undertaker long ago. But the paradox is that they are also symbols of the ideals by which men live. They have fought in the Cause. They have been leaders of the Great Movement. They were heroes in wars, national and social. Hugo served ten years in prison for the Cause. Each in his own way has been apprenticed to the Ideal, and when the Ideal failed he drifted to this Last Resort Saloon where he nourishes his pipe dream and drinks rotgut whisky, waiting for the Big Day. Each in his own way is the complete paradox. Each reveals both sides of the badly minted coin at a single glance. They are the contradiction which is man.

Larry has seen that greed is stronger than any other power in man, that man will "never pay the price of liberty." The whole show is for him a meaningless joke. Hugo has discovered that the proletariat are swine, Oban that his father was a traitor to his son and to the ideals of the state. Harry Hope is constantly defeated and tortured by his loyalty to his friends and the realization of their utterly futile lives.

Each in his turn has developed a pipe dream by which he clings to such shreds of self-respect as are necessary to life. All wait for the turning of the "new leaf" for the "Tomorrow" that never comes, for the ship "loaded to the gunwales with cancelled regrets and promises fulfilled and clean slates and new leases." The "Favoring breeze has the stink of nickel whiskey on its breath. Truth is irrelevant and immaterial. To hell with truth." The whole "misbegotten mad lot" of them is long overdue for the loaded shroud and the green quiet of the bottom of the sea. For them the crows have already made wing to the rocky wood. Night's black angels are approaching for the ultimate feast. Yet they are the symbol of man's humanity.

As the characters are symbols, emphasized and made convincing by the paradox of being outcasts of the lowest order, who under their rags embody the only hope man has in an ideal world, so the place in which they live is made symbolical by the paradox. It is a "morgue wid all de stiffs on deck." The morgue theme is carried throughout the play. The morgue is man's shelter, a place where he is dead or dying or just waiting for death; it is man's world. It is a place from which Harry Hope imagines his dead wife doing "somersaults in her grave" while his companions shake and tremble with "the graveyard fantods." It is the "morgue on a rainy Sunday night," and it is also the "Palace of Pipe Dreams," the shelter where man's last hope for salvation is preserved in cheap whisky. Beneath its filthy exterior, its apparent degradation, lies its complete opposite, the gentle warmth of a home and the tender kindness of Harry Hope.

Into this paradoxical little corner of the world comes the catalytic agent, Hickey, the Iceman of Death, the symbol of salvation, the greatest paradox of all. Into the "Calm atmosphere" of the "Last Harbor," this place as "harmless as a graveyard," where man lives by "the consolation that he hasn't far to go," comes Hickey. This salesman, whose father was a preacher in Indiana, a man of God who sold "Hoosier hayseeds building lots along the Golden Street!" is on first appearance a cheap drummer. He is known for his drinking and carousing, and most of all for his stories, which include lewd references to his wife, Evelyn, and the iceman who consoles her while Hickey is away from home. O'Neill makes him the epitome of the commonplace in order that the paradox which is the essence of tragedy may be the more startling and effective.

Slowly and ingeniously, the opposite Hickey is revealed. The first indication is the remark, "Would Hickey or Death would come." This is emphasized by Hugo's theme of Babylon, and the growing realization that the iceman about whom Hickey has joked is "The Iceman of Death . . . Death was the Iceman Hickey called to his home." This no-account, irresponsible drummer takes on strange forms. The inhabitants of The Last Resort begin to realize that their place, a symbol of man's world, is the antechamber to the morgue, that Larry, the Barker for the Big Sleep, has spoken more truly than he knew.

An ominous atmosphere develops around Hickey as an emissary of Death. Larry says, "I'm damned sure he brought death with him. I could feel the cold touch of him." And later he reaffirms his feeling, "Didn't I tell you he brought death with him?" There is about Hickey "Something not human behind his damned grinning and kidding." Hickey recognizes this feeling and tries to dispel it by saying, "We don't want corpses at this feast." This is a conscious emphasis on the paradox which is the dramatist's problem, for he realizes what the reader only suspects vaguely, that Hickey the Salesman must become the Saviour.

Gradually Hickey's mission becomes clear. He has appeared in a new guise. He has come to save men from their illusions, their pipe dreams. Larry recognizes it first, because he has achieved a semblance of philosophic detachment. He tells his comrades that Hickey has the "miraculous touch to raise the dead." It should have been apparent earlier because as the ending of the first act approaches, Hickey feels the strange power of his message come over him and he urges his potential disciples to, "Let yourself sink down to the bottom of the sea. Rest in peace. There is no further you have to go. Not a single damned hope or dream left to nag you."

Finally his true character appears. Like Jesus he has mystical insight and understanding. He tells Parritt that he knows everything. "You can't hide yourself, not even here on the bottom of the sea." And later to all of them he says, "I know every one of you inside out by heart." Hickey, like the Saviour, recognizes that his time is short.

> I saw I couldn't do what I was after alone. Not in the time at my disposal. I knew when I came here I wouldn't be able to stay with you long. I'm slated to leave on a trip. I saw I'd have to hustle and use every means I could.

His consciousness of being on his Father's business grows upon him, and with it comes that divine certainty which only the God-inspired can have.

> I swear I'd never act like I have if I wasn't absolutely sure it will be worth it to you in the end, after you're rid of the damned guilt . . . and the remorse that nags at you and makes you hide behind lousy pipe dreams about tomorrow. You'll be in a today where there is no yesterday or tomorrow to worry you.

The Scriptural echoes are too familiar to be missed, as is his new term of address "Brothers and Sisters." He will lead them where "no pipe dreams can ever nag at them again."

Before this great affirmation Hickey had told them "You won't be scared of either life or death any more." And Larry had foreseen the end and described it in his account of Harry Hope's birthday party as the "Second feast of Belshazzar with Hickey to do the writing on the wall." He had issued the warning, "Make sure first it's the real McCoy and not poison," a warning that coils around the central theme of all the Saviours who ever came to relieve the self-torture of mankind.

As the play approaches the end the paradox fades. Hickey is no longer a cheap drummer. His mystical qualities are felt in the lives of all the characters. Larry becomes entirely sincere in his deep hatred of "The stupid greed of the human circus." He is weighed down with the ironical pretense of human existence, "The dirty, stinking bit of withered flesh which is my beautiful little life." When Harry Hope comes back from the trial of faith, he feels "all in, like a corpse" and he appears to the others in the same light. He is like Lazarus when he came back from the grave. Hugo notices that Harry looks "Funny. You look dead," and Rocky adds, "He does look like he'd croaked," and Larry recognizes, "It's the peace of death you've brought him."

As the "peace" spreads it works like an active poison in the lives of all the characters. Hugo finds his subconscious speaking out, calling his beloved proletarians "Slaves," and life a crazy monkey face. "Always there is blood beneath the willow trees."

The Saviour who develops must not be construed literally as Jesus. He is just the Saviour, Christ, Buddha, perhaps most of all Lao Tze, for O'Neill has for many years been steeped in the philosophy of the religions of the East. In this play the Saviour is not the Messiah of a particular group but the Saviour of mankind. He embodies the Universal Saviour whose essence is Nihilism. Larry affirms this, telling the others that:

> It's not Bakunin's ghost you ought to pray to in your dreams, but to the great Nihilist, Hickey. He's started a movement that will blow up the world.

What Hickey preaches is the end of all dreams, all the pipe dreams, the end of all "Desire to communicate with the world . . . or . . . to be bothered with its greedy madness." It is the Buddhist's Nirvana, the Christian Heaven, but perhaps most of all the quietism of Lao Tze. It is the peace that comes when man no longer stirs the muddy pool but sits by its edge quietly until the roiled water grows still, the muddy particles settle, and finally the sun goes down, the stars fill the heavens and man is alone, quiet and at peace; beyond desire, pipe dreams, vague hopes and most of all, beyond the futility of actions.

Then, as the end of the play approaches, Hickey must fail, as all Saviours have failed. His magic does not work, his disciples are not happy. They are free from their pipe dreams, but life has lost its savor.

> By rights you should be contented by now, without a single damned hope or lying dream left to torment you! But here you are like a lot of stiffs cheating the undertaker . . . Can't you see there is no tomorrow now?

They are human. They can't live without their ideals and by their ideals they are doomed to torture themselves and each other today, tomorrow and forever as they have throughout their whole miserable and fantastic history. And as Hickey realizes his failure, he welcomes his doom. And the torture returns as his subconscious speaks out his hatred for Evelyn. He had called her a "Damned bitch," and now he must cry out for mercy in his last agony. Death will be the only end to his pipe dream. Larry expresses it, "May the Chair bring him peace at last, the poor tortured bastard."

The curtain falls as the paradox becomes complete. The "saved" actors return to their pipe dreams as men must, as they always have, acting out their part in the antechamber to the morgue. "The days grow hot, O Babylon!" There will be blood beneath the willow trees.

The Iceman and the Bridegroom:
Some Observations on the
Death of O'Neill's Salesman

by Cyrus Day

> While the bridegroom tarried, they all slumbered and slept.
> And at midnight there was a cry made, Behold, the bridegroom
> cometh.
>
> —Matthew 25:5-6

The Iceman Cometh is a play about the death of a salesman; its
central theme is the relationship between men's illusions and their
will to live. The salesman, Theodore Hickman, or Hickey, as he is
called, is a more complex character than Arthur Miller's Willie Loman, and O'Neill's diagnosis of the spiritual *malaise* of the twentieth
century is more profound than Miller's. Loman is depicted from the
outside: he is the victim of a false and wholly external conception
of what constitutes success. He wants, in a worldly sense, to solve the
riddle of life, but the questions he asks are superficial and relatively
easy for an audience or a reader to answer.

Hickey is depicted from the inside. He is more successful as a salesman than Loman, but he is the victim of a far more insidious disease.
He is not versed at first hand (as O'Neill was) in philosophic nihilism, but he has somehow become aware, presumably through a sort of
intellectual osmosis, that modern man no longer believes in objective
reality and truth. Loman is adrift in contemporary American society;
Hickey is adrift in the universe. The difference is a measure of the
difference between O'Neill's aims and the aims of almost all other
modern dramatists.

A few days before *The Iceman Cometh* opened on Broadway in
1946, O'Neill told a reporter that he had tried to express its "deeper"
meaning in its title, and in an interview with S. J. Woolf he said that

"The Iceman and the Bridegroom: Some Observations on the Death of O'Neill's Salesman," by Cyrus Day. From Modern Drama, I *(May, 1958), 3-9. Copyright ⓒ 1958 by* Modern Drama. *Reprinted by permission of the publisher.*

the verb form "cometh" was a "deliberate reference to biblical language." The play itself, he gave Woolf to understand, had religious significance. It is difficult to see what he can have meant by these hints, for *The Iceman Cometh* has few readily discernible connections either with religion or with the Bible. However, since O'Neill was not in the habit of talking at random about his own work, we would do well, if we want to come to terms with the "deeper" meaning of *The Iceman Cometh,* to assume that he had something specific and important in mind, and to try to discover what it was.

O'Neill looked upon himself, we must remember, as a spiritual physician, and he thought that his mission as a dramatist was to "dig at the roots of the sickness of today," which he defined as the death of the old God (echoing Nietzsche) and the failure of science and materialism to provide a new one satisfactory to the remnants of man's primitive religious instincts. Most dramatists write about the relationship between man and man, but he was more interested, he said, in the relationship between man and God. His plays, accordingly, often have a metaphysical basis, but since he had lost his faith in God at an early period in his life, and since he thought that it would take a million years of evolution for man "to grow up and obtain a soul," they are seldom religious in any generally accepted sense of the word.

Days without End, which preceded *The Iceman Cometh,* is an exception. Written in 1934, during a brief period of personal happiness, it is a Christian play. The protagonist, a young man very much like O'Neill himself, is torn by religious doubts, but in the final act he enters a Catholic church, prostrates himself before an image of the crucified Jesus, and becomes at last an integrated personality, at peace with himself and with God. O'Neill, in 1934, appeared to have come to the end of his spiritual pilgrimage.

Actually, *Days without End* was a "mere interlude," as he admitted later, and did not reflect his personal religious convictions. For the moment he may have supposed that he could return to the Christian fold, but by 1939, when he wrote *The Iceman Cometh,* his mood had changed from tentative hope to unqualified despair. World War II was beginning, and the human race was obviously "too damned stupid" (this was O'Neill's phrase) to realize that its salvation depended on one "simple sentence": What shall it profit a man if he gain the whole world and lose his own soul? Perhaps, O'Neill told a reporter, mankind ought to be dumped down the nearest drain and the world given over to the ants.

These are hardly Christian sentiments, despite the quotation from the New Testament, and *The Iceman Cometh* cannot, therefore, have the same sort of religious significance as *Days without End:* it cannot be a Christian play. Can it be a recantation of the point of view of *Days without End?* Can it be, in any sense, a repudiation of Christianity?

Since O'Neill himself has given us the hint, let us begin our inquiry with the title. On the surface, the iceman is a reference to Hickey's ribald jest that he knows his wife is safe because he has left her with the iceman in the hay. On a "deeper" level, the iceman represents death, as O'Neill pointed out in 1946, and as Larry Slade points out in the play when he learns that Hickey's wife is dead. "It fits," Slade says, "for Death was the Iceman Hickey called to his home."

It is not enough, however, merely to identify the iceman with death. We must realize also that the iceman is the foil of the bridegroom of Scripture, and that he stands for the opposite of everything the bridegroom stands for. In the symbolism of theology, the bridegroom is always Christ, giver of life eternal. Waiting for the bridegroom symbolizes man's hope of redemption. Union with the bridegroom, conceived as a marriage, is the "final end and realized meaning" [1] of the life of every Christian, the "fulfillment of promise and [the] consummation of hope." Union with the bridegroom signifies victory over death and salvation in the world to come.

Union with the iceman, conceived as adultery, must, then, be a parody of union with the bridegroom, and signify surrender to death and acquiescence in personal annihilation. Evelyn Hickman, after her husband kills her, finds the peace of oblivion in the arms of the symbolical iceman. The other characters in the play will eventually find the same kind of peace when they abandon their illusory hope of happiness, whether here and now on earth, or in a hypothetical Christian hereafter.

Construed in this way, *The Iceman Cometh* (on one of its many levels of meaning) is seen to be a parable of the destiny of man. All men are waiting for the iceman, but only those who have shed their ultimate illusions are aware that the "final end and realized meaning" of their lives is death. "I'm the only real convert to death Hickey made here," says Slade, who speaks for O'Neill in the play. "From the bottom of my coward's heart I mean that now."

"I want to go to the chair," says Hickey, when he realizes that his love for his wife was an illusion, and that he killed her because he hated her. "Do you suppose I give a damn about life now?" he asks the detective who has arrested him. "Why, you bonehead, I haven't got a single damned lying hope or pipe dream left." The other derelicts in Hope's saloon (the world of illusions) lack Slade's philosophic detachment and Hickey's psychopathic insight, and are afraid to face

---

[1] See L. A. Zander's discussion of the problem of the bridegroom in his *Dostoevsky,* 1948, pp. 97-137.

the truth: that waiting for the iceman constitutes the chief employ-
ment of their futile lives.

The paradox of fulfillment through annihilation is a concept that
O'Neill could have derived either from Schopenhauer or from Freud,
who reached the conclusion previously reached by Schopenhauer,
though by a different route, that the goal of life is death. The immediate stimulus to his imagination, however, may have been Waldo
Frank's novel *The Bridegroom Cometh,* in which the heroine gives
herself to a succession of bridegrooms, both spiritual (Christ, Freud,
Marx) and material (a husband and several lovers). Only Marx satis-
fies her need for love, and in the end she finds fulfillment through
identification with the masses. O'Neill, unlike Frank, never supposed
that a political or sociological nostrum could cure the diseases of the
soul.

A second key to O'Neill's attitude toward Christianity in *The Iceman Cometh* is the role of the hardware salesman Hickey. When the
curtain rises on Act I, the derelicts in Hope's hotel, slumbering and
sleeping in their chairs, are waiting for Hickey to visit them on one
of his periodical benders. "Would that Hickey or Death would come,"
says Willie Oban. But Hickey has tarried: a prostitute has seen him
standing at the next corner, and to her surprise he is sober.

"I kidded him," she says. " 'How's de iceman, Hickey? How's he
doin' at your house?' He laughs and says, 'Fine.' And he says, 'Tell de
gang I'll be along in a minute. I'm just finishin' figurin' out de best
way to save dem and bring dem peace.' "

Hickey, when he arrives, is greeted by a very different cry from
"Behold, the bridegroom cometh." "Here's the old son of a bitch,"
says Rocky; and "Bejees, Hickey, you old bastard, it's good to see
you!" says Hope.

But Hickey is no longer the irresponsible drunkard the derelicts
once knew and loved. He is on the wagon, and he proposes a stern
remedy for what ails them. What he has to sell, in other words, is
symbolical hardware, and he himself represents all self-appointed mes-
siahs and saviors who meddle in other people's affairs and tell them
how to live. Hence he can be fruitfully compared to Gregers Werle
in Ibsen's *Wild Duck,* to Luka in Gorki's *Lower Depths,* and to the
mysterious strangers in Jerome's *Passing of the Third Floor Back* and
Kennedy's *Servant in the House.*

He also has something in common with Sigmund Freud, and his
program of salvation is similar, in a general way, to psychoanalysis.
He invites the derelicts to re-examine their pipe dreams (wish fulfill-
ments) and to get rid of them by coming to terms with reality (the
reality principle). This, he imagines, will make them happy. It doesn't,
of course; and after their abortive attempts to resume their former

occupations, they stagger back, demoralized and defeated, to the security of Hope's saloon. They cannot endure life unsupported by illusions, and instead of making them happy, Hickey deprives them of the will to live. Hickey has the last speech in each of the first three acts, and his last word in each is an ironical "happy." The notion that men can be happy in this worst of all possible worlds is an illusion.

Another illusion, or so Freud tells us, is religion. Man does not need its consolations, he says in *The Future of an Illusion,* nor can he remain a child forever. Rather he must venture out into the hostile world and be educated to reality. "Man can endure the cruelty of reality. What, you fear he will not stand the test? But it is at least something to know that one has been thrown on one's own resources."

This is very much like Hickey's program for the individual derelicts in *The Iceman Cometh.* Over and above their private illusions, however, stands Christianity, the collective illusion of what O'Neill thought of as our bankrupt Western civilization. Religion is an illusion, O'Neill evidently agreed; but unlike Freud, he did not think that the "swine called men" could live without it. Thus, by an extraordinary reconciliation of opposites, he equates the drunken Hickey with the secular savior Freud and the Christian Savior Christ, and at the same time rejects the gospels preached by both. Says Slade:

> Honor or dishonor, faith or treachery, are nothing but the opposites of the same stupidity which is ruler and king of life, and in the end they rot in the same grave. All things are the same meaningless joke to me, for they grin at me from the one skull of death.

That O'Neill had this anti-Christian undertone in mind when he compiled his medley of illusions in *The Iceman Cometh* is further substantiated by several tantalizing resemblances[2] between the play and the New Testament. Hickey as savior has twelve disciples. They drink wine at Hope's supper party, and their grouping on the stage, according to O'Neill's directions, is reminiscent of Leonardo da Vinci's painting of the Last Supper. Hickey leaves the party, as Christ does, aware that he is about to be executed. The three whores correspond in number to the three Marys, and sympathize with Hickey as the three Marys sympathize with Christ. (The implications of this resemblance are not without precedent: Christopher Marlowe, it will be recalled, was accused of saying that the women of Samaria were whores.)

One of the derelicts, Parritt, resembles Judas Iscariot in several ways. He is the twelfth in the list of *dramatis personae;* Judas is twelfth in the New Testament lists of the Disciples. He has betrayed his anarchist mother for a paltry $200; Judas betrayed Christ for

[2] First called to my attention by Mr. Philip Taylor.

thirty pieces of silver. He is from the far-away Pacific Coast; Judas
was from far-away Judaea. Hickey reads his mind and motives; Christ
read Judas's. Parritt compares himself to Iscariot when he says that
his mother would regard anyone who quit the "Movement" as a Judas
who ought to be boiled in oil. He commits suicide by jumping off a
fire escape; Judas fell from a high place (Acts 1:18) or "hanged himself" (Matthew 27:5).

In the light of O'Neill's remarks concerning the Biblical and religious significance of his play, these resemblances can hardly be coin-
cidental. They are no more than an undertone, to be sure—one of
many undertones or subordinate layers of meaning—but they are consistent with the main theme of the play, and they account for some
of its otherwise unaccountable features: for example, the emphasis on
midnight (see Matthew 25:5-6) as the hour appointed for Hope's party,
and the unnecessarily large number of derelicts in Hope's saloon. If
O'Neill's only purpose had been to show that everyone, no matter how
degraded, has one last pipe dream to sustain him, four or five derelicts, instead of twelve, would have sufficed, and the play would have
been less redundant than, in fact, it is.

O'Neill was fond of hidden symbols and multiple layers of meaning.
The nine acts of *Strange Interlude* and the name of the heroine, Nina,
symbolize the nine months of a woman's pregnancy. Christine Mannon
in *Mourning Becomes Electra* is called Christine (to correspond with
Clytemnestra in Aeschylus's trilogy) instead of some other name beginning with "C" because O'Neill wanted to suggest that she is a sort of
female anti-Christ or pagan martyr, crucified by a repressive Puritanism for her faith in sexuality. Lavinia Mannon is called Lavinia instead
of a name beginning with "E" (to correspond with Electra) because
"levin" means lightning or electricity. The name Mannon, from the
last part of Agamemnon, suggests Mammon, the figurative divinity of
all genuine Mannons. Examples of this sort of ingenuity, culled from
other plays by O'Neill, could be multiplied indefinitely.

In addition to Hickey and Christine Mannon, O'Neill likens several
other characters to Christ. In *The Fountain,* Bishop Menendez advises
Juan to surrender the Indian Nano to the mob.

Juan (*with wild scorn*). Ah, High Priest! Deliver him up, eh?
Menendez. Juan! You are impious! (*Angrily*) It is sacrilege—to compare
   this Indian dog—you mock our Blessed Savior! You are cursed—I wash
   my hands—His will be done!

Nina, in *Strange Interlude,* cherishes the illusion that her dead lover
Gordon Shaw is the real father of her son. "Immaculate conception,"

Marsden mutters in an unpublished manuscript version of the play.[3] "The Sons of the Father have all been failures!" Nina says, referring both to her son and to Christ. "Failing, they died for us . . . they could not stay with us, they could not give us happiness."

Allusions such as these abound in O'Neill's plays. *Where the Cross Is Made,* to cite a final example, contains what I surmise is a double reference to the sustaining power of illusions (the central theme, as we have seen, of *The Iceman Cometh*). As the curtain falls on the last scene, Nat Bartlett cries out with insane frenzy: "The treasure is buried where the cross is made." On the surface, this means that Nat, like his father, is obsessed by the belief that the trinkets on the island represent a fortune in gold. But the words also suggest that Christianity, symbolized by the Cross, is as much of an illusion as the gold. In view of the way he worked and thought, O'Neill cannot have been unaware of this implication of his title.

These considerations bring to mind an ironic scene in *The Great God Brown.* Dion Anthony, one of O'Neill's favorite characters and a recognizable self-portrait, designs a cathedral which, he boasts, is "one vivid blasphemy from the sidewalk to the tips of the spires!—but so concealed the fools will never know! They'll kneel and worship the ironic Silenus who tells them the best good is never to be born!"

When Brown inherits Dion's soul, he too introduces secret motifs into his work. Of a new state capitol that he designs, he says:

> Here's a wondrous fair Capitol! The design would do just as well for a Home for Criminal Imbeciles! Yet to them, such is my art, it will appear to possess a pure common sense, a fat-bellied finality, as dignified as the suspenders of an assemblyman. Only to me will that pompous façade reveal itself as the wearily ironic grin of Pan as he half listens to the laws passed by his fleas to enslave him.

Did O'Neill, in writing *The Iceman Cometh*—the question inevitably presents itself—did O'Neill do what Dion and Brown do in *The Great God Brown?* Did he, that is to say, introduce concealed blasphemies into his play, just as Dion and Brown introduce concealed blasphemies into their architectural designs? And did he laugh in secret at the critics who supposed that he had written a compassionate play in *The Iceman Cometh,* just as Dion and Brown laugh at the fools who do not see through their mockery?

André Malraux once asked if man in the twentieth century could survive after God had died in the nineteenth. O'Neill's answer in *The*

---

[3] Yale MS. 52, not at present available to scholars, but discussed by Miss Doris Alexander in her brilliant doctoral thesis entitled *Freud and O'Neill: An Analysis of Strange Interlude* (New York University, 1952).

Iceman Cometh is no. The derelicts in Hope's saloon, all of them childless, symbolize a humanity that is engaged in the laudable act of committing suicide. As the play ends, Larry Slade stares straight ahead (O'Neill's habitual way of depicting disillusionment) and waits for release from the intolerable burden of life. O'Neill's prolonged search for a faith had led him, not to faith, but to despair.

Could there have been in 1939, a more prophetic anticipation of the self-destructive compulsions of the Age of Nuclear Fission? Is there in dramatic literature a more nihilistic play than *The Iceman Cometh*?

The Iceman Cometh

by Doris Falk

In 1939, six years after *Days Without End,* O'Neill completed *The Iceman Cometh,* in 1940-41, *Long Day's Journey Into Night,* and in 1943, *A Moon for the Misbegotten* and *A Touch of the Poet.* During the same general period—from about 1934 to 1943—O'Neill had been hard at work on two long cycles of plays to be called *A Tale of Possessors Self-Dispossessed* and *By Way of Obit.* Of the first cycle he completed first drafts of three double-length plays, *The Greed of the Meek, And Give Me Death,* and *More Stately Mansions.* Dissatisfied with the early drafts of these plays and too ill to undertake drastic revision, O'Neill destroyed the first two. Although he had intended the destruction also of *More Stately Mansions,* a typescript of that play survives (the manuscript version was destroyed with the other two plays). Of the second cycle, *By Way of Obit,* O'Neill completed only one one-act play, entitled *Hughie,* still extant but unpublished.

At one time O'Neill had placed *A Touch of the Poet* fifth in the *Possessors* cycle, but when he abandoned the latter he considered his last four plays to be a related series, arranged in the following order: *The Iceman Cometh, A Moon for the Misbegotten, A Touch of the Poet,* and *Long Day's Journey Into Night.* The exact composition dates of these and the cycle plays are far from clear; some had begun years before—*A Touch of the Poet* in 1928. We do know, however, that between completion of *Days Without End* and this final group of plays about ten years had elapsed in which O'Neill's thinking underwent a change that reflected the frustrations of the intervening years.

O'Neill returned in these last plays to acceptance of struggle and flight as inseparable from and intrinsic to the life process. Now there is no way out but death. The struggle in these plays is essentially the same as it had always been in his work: the conscious intellect at war with the unconscious drives, the laceration of love and hate in every

"The Iceman Cometh" (*Original title: "Fatal Balance"*). *From* Eugene O'Neill and the Tragic Tension, *by Doris Falk (New Brunswick, N.J.: Rutgers University Press, 1958), pp. 156-64. Copyright © 1958 by Rutgers, the State University. Reprinted by permission of the publisher.*

close human relationship, and the desperate search for self among the masks. Flight from the struggle is still in the pursuit of one of these illusory masks—but here we see a difference.

At last O'Neill had come face to face with the inevitable question: What happens when, long before the end of the play, the fugitive becomes clearly conscious that flight is futile and the self-image false? When he learns that *all* self-images are illusions, and that furthermore they are projected by a self which is worthless, if it exists at all? Then the self and its ideal are equal—and both equal to zero. Instead of a pull from the self to the self-conception, resulting in action (wasteful though that action may be), we have a perfect equilibrium, resulting in paralysis. Then, indeed,

> . . . the odds is gone,
> And there is nothing left remarkable
> Beneath the visiting moon.

The theme of *The Iceman Cometh* is the death that results—the "iceman" who comes—when the self-images which keep the characters alive become known to them as mirage. The action takes place in "Hope's back room," the back room and a section of the bar of Harry Hope's saloon. Here fifteen derelicts keep themselves alive on alcohol and the "pipe dream" that they have been or some day will be respectable. They all know, at least unconsciously, the truth about themselves and each other, but they know, too, the vital necessity of illusion. So each accepts the other at his own evaluation and demands the same acceptance. As long as this state of things persists, as it does throughout the first act (nearly half the play), the characters are treated as comic. Their self-deceptions are ridiculous but not unlovable affectations. It is in the second act that, as O'Neill said, "the comedy breaks up and the tragedy comes on."

The commentator on the action and the actual protagonist of the play is Larry Slade, an aging ex-Anarchist who has long since withdrawn from the Movement and from life. In Act I Larry is comparatively happy. He has an image of himself as the philosopher-bum who observes life from the grandstand and waits only for death. He is proud that he can see what the others cannot: that "the lie of a pipedream is what gives life to the whole misbegotten mad lot of us, drunk or sober. . . . Mine are all dead and buried behind me. What's before me is the comforting fact that death is a fine long sleep and I'm damned tired, and it can't come too soon for me." (Act I, *Plays*, III, p. 578.)

Yet, Larry's final disillusionment is still to come, in the person of young Parritt, the eighteen-year-old ex-Anarchist who has betrayed the Movement and his own mother, whom Larry once loved. (In fact,

the context hints that Parritt is Larry's son.) Disillusion comes for
the others in the person of Hickey (Theodore Hickman), the traveling
salesman whose success they all envy.

Hickey arrives at the bar on Harry Hope's birthday, an occasion for
one of his periodical binges, but instead of the gay and dissolute
Hickey they all expect, he is serious and sober. He announces the
reason for the change: He has at last found peace by facing the truth
about himself. Gradually he shames his listeners into believing that
they, too, will find peace if they destroy their illusions and see themselves as they really are. He persuades all except Larry to go forth into
the daylight and attempt the social rehabilitation they have always
promised themselves. One by one, however, they crawl back to the
bar the next day, broken and defeated by inevitable failure. They
have faced the truth, but it has robbed them of the last, pitiful trace
of hope.

Now not even liquor can make them happy; their old friendships
turn to antagonisms. Hickey realizes that his plan has failed, and in
trying to explain the failure to himself and to them he reveals that he
attained his state of "peace" by killing his wife, Evelyn.

Hickey has convinced himself that he killed his wife because he
loved her and wanted to spare her unhappiness over his uncontrolla-
ble drunkenness and dissipation—but as he speaks, his real motive
comes through. He hated Evelyn because no matter what he did she
always forgave him, never punished him, was always faithful. His
running gag with the boys at Hope's had been that Evelyn was be-
traying him "in the hay with the iceman," but this was only his own
wishful thinking. She never gave him even this relief from his own
guilt. Hickey killed Evelyn because that was the only way he could
free himself from her eternal forgiveness and achieve the ultimate
in self-punishment. For him, to commit murder was to commit suicide.
He has already called the police at the time of his confession.

When the police have arrived, however, and Hickey is concluding
his story, his guilt becomes too much for him to face. Ironically, he
creates his own pipe dream by persuading himself that he was insane
at the moment of the murder. Hickey's illusion is a blessing to his
friends, for it restores their own. Now they can go back to their bot-
tles, convinced that they knew Hickey was insane all the time and
faced reality only to humor him.

But Larry cannot go back. He must listen to Parritt's confessions—
in dramatic antiphony to Hickey's—of his hatred of his mother
(caused chiefly by jealousy of her many lovers) which led him to be-
tray her to life imprisonment. Parritt has already resolved upon suicide, but he forces Larry to support his resolution. After listening to
Parritt's outpourings, Larry finally cries, "Go, get the hell out of life,

God damn you, before I choke it out of you! . . ." Parritt is relieved
and grateful: "Thanks, Larry. I just wanted to be sure. I can see now
it's the only possible way I can ever get free from her. . . . It ought
to comfort Mother a little, too. . . . She'll be able to say, 'Justice is
done! So may all traitors die!' . . ."

The mother-spirit has destroyed another of her sons.

When Larry hears Parritt fall from the fire escape, "A long forgotten
faith returns to him for a moment. . . ." At least Parritt had the
courage of his conviction. But the death of Parritt is the death of
Larry's last illusion about himself. "He opens his eyes—with a bitter
self-derision." He is no longer the philosopher, but only another
down-and-out bum.

> Be God, there's no hope! I'll never be a success in the grandstand—or
> anywhere else! Life is too much for me! I'll be a weak fool looking
> with pity at the two sides of everything till the day I die! . . . Be God,
> I'm the only real convert to death Hickey made here. From the bottom
> of my coward's heart I mean that now! (Act IV, *Plays*, III, pp. 726-727.)

The objectivist (as Larry thought he was at first), who looks at
both sides of everything until they have equal value, must be a
paralyzed spectator, unable to take action in any direction; but when
the "two sides" are the masks of himself and both are worthless illusions, perfectly balanced against each other, he is not even a paralyzed
spectator; he is dead. In *The Iceman Cometh*, as in the earlier plays,
life and the self are lost together, when the tragic tension between the
selves is lost.

The two sides of himself that Larry has seen are his expansive and
submissive self-images. The expansive is that of the Anarchist, the
active participator in "the Movement." The submissive is seen in his
drive toward self-destruction. If Larry had been able to give either
of these selves the value of a reality, he would have been drawn toward one or toward the other, would have been able to act either in
the direction of his political obligations or in the direction of death
by suicide, as Parritt did. Since he is pulled in both directions at once,
he can only withdraw from the struggle altogether and become a non-
participating observer of himself as well as of life. In Jung's terms,
Larry exemplifies the "equal distribution of psychic energy." In
Horney's, he is the neurotic who finds a pseudosolution to conflict in
"resignation: the appeal of freedom." When Larry himself discovers
the unreality of his solution, there is nothing left for him but the living death which Kierkegaard called "the disconsolateness of not being
able to die." Even his conception of physical death as a warm and
comforting womb (the return to the Earth Mother) or as a Babylon
where " 'tis cool beneath thy willow tree" is to him only another illu-

sion. Nevertheless, death is the single solution to his dilemma, since only annihilation of the self can annihilate the dilemma. His very inability to propel himself actively toward this annihilation—to accomplish it through suicide—is also death.

The philosophical implications of Larry's position are just as interesting as the psychological. Behind Aristotle's ethical definition of character as "that which reveals moral purpose, showing what kind of things a man chooses or avoids," is the problem which exists in some degree for every self-aware person, as it does in the extreme for the neurotic: the problem of creating oneself, of forming one's own character. The preliminaries and the process of choosing, even though they may be unconscious, are as important as the choice itself and the responsibility which is its result. Larry's power of choice is brought to a standstill because he cannot accomplish the preparation for it. His is the problem of projecting value in a world devoid of absolutes —the "existential" dilemma: man's chief struggle is not with Something but with Nothing, not with Evil but with the valuelessness that is neither good nor evil. Once he has overcome this Nothing, has created his values, man is then free to act according to them (or even, knowingly, contrary to them), but he is completely responsible both for the values and the actions predicated upon them. Such utter self-contingency can be paralyzing; it provides freedom, but it is that terrifying freedom from which, as Erich Fromm points out, most of us feel compelled to escape.

In defense of this philosophy as a "humanism" Sartre has pointed out that it is as positive as it is negative—as hopeful as it is despairing —in that each man has not only the responsibility, but the opportunity, to create his own destiny, and that each individual is ultimately responsible for the destiny of mankind as a whole. O'Neill has not only placed Larry in the existential dilemma, but has made him see and live both sides of the dilemma itself. In his youth Larry dedicated himself to Anarchism, an affirmation of nothingness and chaos and of man's freedom to create his destiny; but in his old age he sees anarchy's opposite face, that negation which we call despair.

The Iceman Cometh

by Robert Brustein

In *Ah Wilderness!*, romanticized sex and half-baked philosophy, finally, are the enthusiasms of a character who is an adolescent himself; and, as a result, the play marks a turning point in O'Neill's relation to his material. If *Days Without End* suggests a new detachment towards his religious questing, *Ah Wilderness!* prefigures his transformation into an objective dramatic artist. As his self-awareness grows, O'Neill is beginning to distance himself from dogma and opinions. In the mouth of the seventeen-year-old Romantic Richard Miller, the author's familiar paeans to Beauty, Love, and Life seem perfectly acceptable, since O'Neill is treating these affirmations with gentle satire and indulgent whimsey. It is the character, not the author, who is now identified with *fin de siècle* pessimism, culled from Swinburne, Nietzsche, and Omar Khayyam, just as it is the character, not the author, who is inclined to sentimentalize prostitutes. The play, in short, has finally become more important than the theme—ideas are effectively subordinated to "the experience in which they are implied." By projecting his literary self-consciousness onto an earlier Self, O'Neill is beginning to free himself from it. And in *Ah Wilderness!*, he exposes previously suppressed talents for depicting the habitual and commonplace side of existence, along with unsuspected gifts for portraying the humorous side of Irish family life.

Ah Wilderness!, to be sure, is an exercise for the left hand—a sentimental piece of Americana written in a holiday mood—but it is less important in itself than for what it portends: O'Neill is preparing to strike out along new paths. The author himself seems perfectly conscious of a new departure in this play, because, in a letter to Lawrence Langner, he couples it with *Days Without End* as evidence of his growing self-understanding: "For, after all, this play [*Days Without End*], like *Ah Wilderness!* but in a much deeper sense, is the paying of an old debt on my part—a gesture toward more compre-

hensive, unembittered understanding and inner freedom—the breaking away from an old formula that I had enslaved myself with. . . ."
What the "old formula" is we have already seen; O'Neill's new approach is to leave all formulae behind, and relax into the role of the
artist. Psychologically, O'Neill's bitterness towards authority seems
to have left him, along with his restless quest for absolutes; philosophically, he has begun to perceive the hollowness of his messianic
pretensions, and to turn towards material which he has pulled out of
his being rather than self-consciously adopted; thematically, he has
abandoned myths of incest and romantic love for deeper probes of
character; formally, he is learning to combine the solipsistic subjec-
tivity of Strindberg with the more detached, ordered, and indirectly
biographical approach of Ibsen. Instead of writing about his unas-
similated present, O'Neill is beginning to root about in the experiences of his past, and to do so with patience and care. After producing at least one play a year from 1913 to 1933 (in 1920, he wrote
four), O'Neill considerably slows his output, completing only four
full-length works and one short play in the next twenty years.

 Ah Wilderness! is like all the plays which are to follow in being a
work of recollection—nostalgic and retrospective. And significantly,
it does not contain a trace of Expressionism, being surprisingly conventional in technique and structure. Later, O'Neill is to develop a
different kind of realism all his own, built on a centripetal pattern in
which a series of repetitions bring us closer and closer to the explosion
at the center; but *Ah Wilderness!* is typical of O'Neill's late plays in
its avoidance of conspicuous formal experimentation. Masks, split
characters, and choruses are gone forever. As a result, O'Neill aban-
dons those ponderous abstractions and inflated generalizations which
Expressionism invariably dragged into his plays. If the author once
complained, about *The Hairy Ape,* that "the public saw just the
stoker, not the symbol, and the symbol makes the play either important or just another play," then he is now able to subordinate symbolism, and sometimes suppress it entirely for the sake of penetrating
studies of character.

 O'Neill, in short, has finally discovered where his true talents lie.
In 1924, in the act of eulogizing Strindberg, he had called Ibsen a
"lesser man," attacking Ibsenite realism in these terms: "It represents
our Fathers' daring aspirations towards self-recognition by holding the
family kodak up to ill-nature . . . we have endured too much from
the banality of surfaces." Less embittered towards "our Fathers"
nine years later, O'Neill is beginning to create a drama of surface
banality himself—beneath which the forces of destruction will proceed with Ibsenite inevitability—and it is precisely the "family
kodak" which will be O'Neill's artistic instrument. As John Henry

Raleigh has observed about one of these late plays, "Everything pales beside the fact of the *family*, which is the macro-microcosm that blots out the universe. . . ." The family becomes the nucleus of every major work that follows, except *The Iceman Cometh*, and even there, the characters are thrown together into a kind of accidental family group. As for the unfinished cycle, this was inspired by O'Neill's desire to follow his family further and further into the past: "The Cycle is primarily that," he writes to Langner, "the history of a family. What larger significance I can give my people as extraordinary examples and symbols in the drama of American possessiveness and materialism is something else again." In *Ah Wilderness!*, O'Neill develops a hazy daguerreotype of Irish family life at the turn of the century; but before long, the family kodak will focus on the author's most painful early memories, seen with consuming power and ruthless honesty, yet with compassion, understanding, and love.

O'Neill's retrospective technique is admirably illustrated in *The Iceman Cometh* (1939), where O'Neill closes the door forever on his messianic ambitions, and the suffering artist becomes completely identified with the structured art. "*The Iceman* is a denial of any other experience of faith in my plays," he remarks, soon after completing the play. "In writing it, I felt I had locked myself in with my memories." At first glance, the author's place in these memories is obscure, for the play does not look very autobiographical. Harry Hope's saloon is based on Jimmy-the-Priest's, a West-Side rooming bar that O'Neill used to frequent in his youth—("Gorky's Night Lodgings," he was later to remark, "was an ice cream parlor in comparison," and the influence of Gorky is certainly evident in the seedy, peeled, splotched setting, and the dissipated characters)[1] and the play contains thinly veiled portraits of some of the derelicts the author used to know there and at another saloon called the Hell Hole. But although the work is set in 1912, the same climacteric year as *A Long Day's Journey*, the author himself is simply a lens through which the characters are seen. Still, if O'Neill is not the central character of the play, romanticized as a mocking, sardonic rebel, he is still present in disguise—partly in two characters, as we shall see, but mostly as a guide through the caverns of his deepest perceptions. O'Neill here is using his "memories" not for personal autobiography in the manner of Strindberg, but in the manner of Ibsen, for spiritual and psychological autobiography. As the author himself says, *The Iceman Cometh* is a repudiation of "any other experience of faith in

[1] For an analysis of Gorky's influence on the play, see Helen Muchnic's article, "The Irrelevancy of Belief: The Iceman and the Lower Depths," in *O'Neill and His Plays*, edited by Oscar Cargill, N. Bryllion Fagin, and William J. Fisher.

my plays." In denying his previous philosophical affirmations, he permits a terrible sense of reality to rise to consciousness.

In its repudiation of past faith, *The Iceman Cometh* occupies much the same place in O'Neill's work as *The Wild Duck* does in Ibsen's; and, indeed, the two plays have more in common even than this positioning. The theme of *The Iceman*—that men cannot live without illusions—is so close to the theme of *The Wild Duck*[2] that some critics have been inclined to dismiss the later play as a mere recapitulation of the earlier one. This is a mistake. O'Neill's play, to my mind, is a greater achievement than Ibsen's, and it certainly has a different emphasis. In *The Wild Duck,* it is morally wrong to rob people of their life-lies; in *The Iceman Cometh,* it is *tragic.* Gregers Werle is a satire on pseudo-Ibsenites who meddle in the lives of others, urging the claim of some impossible ideal, but Theodore Hickman is not a vicarious idealist but a realist, and one who believes he has pragmatically tested the kind of salvation he is pressing on his friends. Although Gregers is misguided, and Hjalmar Ekdal is inadequate to his demands, Ibsen still believes there are heroic individuals (Brand and Stockman, for example) with the courage to face the unclothed truth. But the whole world is inadequate to Hickey's demands, for the truth he offers is a naked, blinding light which kills. Thus, *The Wild Duck* is a savage indictment of some men; *The Iceman Cometh* is a compassionate insight into all. O'Neill is reflecting not ethically, on Right Action or Right Thought, but metaphysically, on the very quality of existence. And, as a result, he is finally working through experientially to that tragic mood so self-consciously imposed on his earlier work.

Because he is universalizing Ibsen's theme, O'Neill has created instead of one antagonist a whole catalogue of them—the deadbeats, alcoholics, pimps, whores, bartenders, and illusionists who inhabit Harry Hope's premises. The proliferation of characters adds greatly to the length of the play, which is bulky and unwieldy in the extreme; and since each character is identified by a single obsession which he continually restates, the play is extremely repetitious as well. Thus, despite the naturalistic setting, the play is much too schematic to qualify as a convincing evocation of reality. Each act offers a single variation on the theme of illusion; the action never bursts into spontaneous life; and the characters rarely transcend their particular functions. A thematic realism rather than an atmospheric realism prevails; O'Neill seems reluctant to let the play escape his rigid control. One

[2] It is also very close to the theme of Pirandello's plays, though O'Neill differs from the Italian dramatist in believing that objective reality can still be reached through the human mind.

must concede that there is some justice in Eric Bentley's objection:
"There are ideas in the play, and we have the impression that what
should be the real substance of it is mere (not always deft) contrivance to illustrate the ideas." Still, O'Neill's ideas, for once, proceed
logically from the action, and, for once, they are totally convincing. I
do not think Professor Bentley properly appreciates the depth, sincerity, and relevance of O'Neill's dramatic insights in this play.

Professor Bentley detects padding and recommends cuts; O'Neill's
Broadway director, Paul Crabtree, also suggested cuts on the basis
that O'Neill has made the same point eighteen times—"I intended
to be repeated eighteen times," the playwright said, and refused to
tamper with the play. O'Neill was right; cutting would undoubtedly
diminish the impact of the work. For once, an O'Neill play is long not
because the author knows too little but rather because he knows too
much; even the repetitions are an intricate aspect of the total design.
O'Neill has multiplied his antagonists in order to illuminate every
aspect of his theme, just as he has drawn them from the humblest
condition of life in order to show mankind at the extremity of its fate.
Dazed by alcohol, isolated from human society, O'Neill's derelicts
are stripped of every pretension except the single "pipe dream" that
keeps them going, and the sum of these pipe dreams is meant to
represent the total content of human illusion.

Thus, Hugo's aristocratic will to power through pretended love of
the proletariat reflects on political illusions; Joe's pugnacious demand
for equality with the whites, on racial illusions; Chuck and Cora's
fantasy of marriage and a farm, on domestic illusions; the prostitutes'
mysterious distinction between "tarts" and "whores," on status illusions; Parritt's false motives for having betrayed his mother, on
psychological illusions; Willie Oban's excuse for having discontinued
law school, on intellectual illusions; Larry Slade's pretense at disillusionment and detachment, on philosophical illusions—and Hickey's
belief that he has found salvation, on religious illusions. All of these
dreamers represent a family of men, inextricably bound up with each
other. Each is able to see the lie of the other without being able to
admit his own, but in this community, the price of mutual toleration
is mutual silence. Actually, the community is almost Utopian. Before
Hickey comes, the men live in relative harmony together by adhering
to a single doctrine—the doctrine of Tomorrow—keeping hope alive
through the anticipation of significant action on a day which never
comes.

Against the Tomorrow doctrine, Hickey counterposes his doctrine
of Today, forcing the derelicts to execute their dreams—and fail
them—on the assumption that a life without illusions is a life without
guilt. In this conflict of ideologies, Hickey's main antagonist is Larry

Slade, the intellectual champion of the Tomorrowmen, who is brought
into the lists against his conscious will. Playing the part of the "Old
Grandstand Foolosopher," pretending indifference to the fate of his
companions, Larry has adopted a mask of total alienation. For him,
the essence of mankind is excrement, and life on earth is doomed:
"The material the ideal society must be constructed from is men
themselves," he observes, explaining his apostasy from Anarchism,
"and you can't build a marble temple out of mud and manure." "Old
Cemetery," as he is called, is aroused only by the thought of death,
and affects to contemplate his own with pleasurable anticipation. But
although he pretends "a bitter, cynic philosophy," as Jimmy Tomorrow observes, "in your heart, you are the kindest man among us."
Actually, Larry is doomed to inaction by a reflective intelligence
which always sees both sides of a question, and he is forever trying
to suppress his instinctive compassion. O'Neill describes him as "a
pitying but weary old priest." He has heard all the secrets of the con-
fessional, and out of his secret kindness is desperately trying to protect these secrets, including his own, from Hickey's remorseless efforts
to bring them into light. Harry Hope's may be "Bedrock Bar, The
End of the Line Cafe, The Bottom of the Sea Rathskeller," but it has
"a beautiful calm in the atmosphere" which can only be preserved if
it is not touched by truth.

Hickey, however, finds this a false calm, and desires to introduce
a genuine spiritual peace: "All I want," he says, using a word which
ironically concludes every act but the last, "is to see you *happy*." But
while Hickey is convinced that only truth brings peace, Larry knows
that happiness is based exclusively on mutual deception: "To hell
with the truth! As the history of the world proves, the truth has no
bearing on anything. . . . The lie of a pipe dream is what gives life
to the whole misbegotten mad lot of us, drunk or sober." This tension
between truth and illusion reflects, in much stronger dramatic terms,
O'Neill's former antithesis of Nietzschean heroism and Christian
compassion. But instead of forcing a synthesis, as he does in his messianic plays, O'Neill rejects the heroic teachings of Nietzsche, re-
pudiating superhuman salvation while affirming humanity, pity, and
love. Together, Hickey and Larry function in somewhat the same way
as the split characters of O'Neill's earlier work; but having relin-
quished his messianic claims, O'Neill is able to treat both aspects of
his personality with a good deal more balance and equanimity. Thus,
Larry's facile pessimism, his cynicism, and his fascination with death
are all qualities found in O'Neill's earlier "sardonic" heroes, but
these are now exposed as mere attitudinizing. And Hickey's evangelism represents the messianic impulse in O'Neill turned back on itself,
for his gospel of truth is revealed as the greatest illusion of all.

The Iceman Cometh, then, is about the impossibility of salvation in a world without God, an expression of existential revolt structured in quasi-religious terms. And beneath the realistic surface, O'Neill is developing an ironic Christian parable, in a surprisingly subtle manner. For one thing, Hickey's entrance is delayed so long that—like another long-awaited figure, Beckett's Godot—he begins to accumulate supernatural qualities. "Would that Hickey or Death would come," moans one impatient character—an anticipatory irony, since Hickey will soon be identified with Death. Hickey finally does arrive, but the amiable jester has undergone a startling transformation. "I'm damned sure he's brought death with him," remarks Larry. "I feel the cold touch of it on him." The recurrent iceman motif intensifies these associations. On each of his annual visits, Hickey has joked that his chaste wife, Evelyn, was in the hay with the iceman; and as the derelicts grow more and more tormented by Hickey's penetrating thrusts, their one hope is that the joke has come to roost. And indeed it has, though not in the manner they think. Evelyn is now being held in a frigid embrace; Hickey, we finally learn, has murdered her; "Death was the Iceman Hickey called to his home." Thus, Hickey, Death, and the Iceman are one. The truth doesn't set you free, it kills you dead; the peace which Hickey brings to Harry Hope's saloon is the peace of the grave. Hickey, therefore, is the false Messiah—not the Resurrection and the Life, but the "great Nihilist," starting "a movement which will blow up the world."

To emphasize his anti-messianic point, O'Neill has hidden parallels with another great world movement, Christianity, throughout the play. And Cyrus Day has done us the service of uncovering most of them in his article, "The Iceman and the Bridegroom":

> Hickey as savior has twelve disciples. They drink wine at Hope's supper party, and their grouping on the stage, according to O'Neill's directions, is reminiscent of Leonardo da Vinci's painting of the Last Supper. Hickey leaves the party, as Christ does, aware that he is about to be executed. The three whores correspond in number to the three Marys, and sympathize with Hickey as the three Marys sympathize with Christ. . . . One of the derelicts, Parritt, resembles Judas Iscariot in several ways. He is twelfth in the list of dramatis personae; Judas is twelfth in the New Testament of the Disciples. He has betrayed his anarchist mother for a paltry $200; Judas betrayed Christ for thirty pieces of silver. . . .

To this list of striking resemblances, we might add another interesting one. Larry Slade becomes the only real convert to Hickey's religion of Death—he is, like Saint Peter, the rock on which Hickey builds his Church.

The symbolic aspect of the play, however, is not very obtrusive, if indeed it is noticeable at all without the aid of a commentator. On a purely denotative level, the work is still very rich. O'Neill has carefully combined Hickey's symbolic role as a false Messiah with his family background and psychological history, so that Hickey stands as a full-bodied character on his own, and a much more convincing salesman figure than Miller's Willy Loman (at least we know what Hickey sells—hardware). The son of a minister, Hickey has brought an evangelical fervor to the drummer's trade, and the techniques of salesmanship to his evangelism. In a country where everything is bought and sold, O'Neill is suggesting, even a religious vision must be peddled. Bruce Barton's observation that Jesus was a super-salesman may be in the back of O'Neill's mind; Billy Graham's religious "crusades" come immediately to ours. Hickey certainly employs the "hard sell"—cheery, good-humored, loud, brash, and pitiless—bearing down on his victim like Major Barbara bringing God to Bill Walker, or a psychoanalyst unearthing the source of a patient's neurosis. He has an instinctual eye for human weakness, partly because of his own experience ("I've had hell inside me. I can spot it in others"), but partly because he is "The Great Salesman" and can detect the vulnerability of a client in an instant.

As a result of this native shrewdness, Hickey has, by the end of the second act, transformed all the derelicts into caged animals, snarling at each other in their agony: each is beginning to open the other's wounds in order to protect his own, and even the goodnatured Harry Hope has developed an uncharacteristic pugnacity. Torn from the security of their dreams, the derelicts must now confront their Tomorrow, each performing the deed which terrifies him most. The third act takes place in cold, daylight horror. The derelicts are afflicted with the "katzenjammers," their withdrawal symptoms aggravated by a growing apprehensiveness. Harry Hope, symbolizing the communal predicament, prepares at last to walk around the ward—but is unable even to cross the street. His illusion exposed, Harry's hope vanishes, and with it the hope of all his companions: only blank, unstructured reality remains. Having abandoned hope, the men are dwelling in hell; even the alcohol has lost its punch; all escape routes are closed. What results is death-in-life: "Vhat's matter, Harry?" asks Hugo. "You look funny. You look dead." Hugo's babbling, and the growling of the derelicts, turns the atmosphere funereal. Hickey's salvation is failing, and so is Hickey's confidence: "That's what worries me about you, Governor," he says to Harry, as the expected peace fails to come. "It's time you began to feel happy—"

In the last act, the derelicts have turned to stone, their spirits calcified by the death ray of truth. Motivated by growing nervousness over their behavior, Hickey begins his long speech of confession—

a confession which is also a discovery—paralleled by an antiphonal speech from Parritt. Both have destroyed a woman; both for reasons that they cannot face. Parritt has informed on his mother not out of patriotism or penury but rather out of hatred; and Hickey has killed Evelyn because she killed his joy of life, filling him with guilt through constant forgiveness of his sins. Thus, Hickey's act was an act of revenge and not of love; he not only hated her illusion, he detested her. As he blurts out, in the unconsidered slip which gives him away, "You know what you can do with your pipe dream now, you damned bitch."

Hickey can admit this feeling to his consciousness only for a moment; then, he immediately pleads insanity. "Good God, I couldn't have said that! If I did, I'd gone insane! Why, I loved Evelyn better than anything in life." It is this plea which leads Eric Bentley to say that "O'Neill's eye was off the subject":

> Not being clearly seen, the man is unclearly presented to the audience; O'Neill misleads them for several hours, then asks them to reach back into their memory and re-interpret all Hickey's actions and attitudes from the beginning. Is Hickey the character O'Neill needed as the man who tries to deprive the gang of their illusions? He (as it turns out) is a maniac. But if the attempt to disillude the gang is itself mad, it would have more dramatic point made by a sane idealist (as in *The Wild Duck*).

I cite this passage because it contains a widely shared misunderstanding of the play which has obscured its real profundity. For the fact is, of course, that O'Neill's eye remained steadfastly on the subject: Hickey, consistent in conception from first to last, is not a maniac at all. Actually, he only claims to have been insane at the time of the murder, but even this is a self-deception which he adopts so as not to face his real feelings towards his wife. Such a conclusion is clear enough from the context, and Parritt suggests it even more bluntly in the course of his own confession: *"And I'm not putting up any bluff either, that I was crazy afterwards* when I laughed to myself and thought, 'You know what you can do with your freedom pipe dream now, don't you, you damned old bitch!' "* [My emphasis]. Hickey's plea of insanity, in short, is a bluff—not to escape the chair (he wants to die now) but to escape the truth: he cannot admit that he hated his wife. In a context like this, as a matter of fact, Hickey's mental state is totally irrelevant, since even madness is an escape from an unpleasant reality; the point is that Hickey, who thought he was living the truth, was living another pipe dream. As for the derelicts, they are willing to believe that Hickey was mad, because this means he told them lies; if he will agree to let them have their illusions, they will agree to let him have his. Hickey hesitates because he knows he told them the truth, but for the sake of his own peace, he must agree to the trade. Thus, he enters their community at last: mutual toleration through mutual silence.

Hickey's brand of salvation, in short, has proved of false manufacture: the happiness he discovered after Evelyn's death was merely the happiness of another illusion. Thus, his attempt to "disillude the gang" is not "itself mad," it is simply based on a terrible error; and since his own illusions are directly implicated in the action, Hickey has a good deal *more* dramatic point than Gregers Werle. Hickey, in fact, has some of the dimension of a tragic protagonist, and is brought right up to the brink of a tragic perception; if he does not look over, then Larry Slade does, and what he sees is the bottomless abyss of a totally divested reality:

> Be God, there's no hope. I'll never be a success in the grandstand—or anywhere else! Life is too much for me! I'll be a weak fool looking with pity at the two sides of everything till the day I die! (*With an intense bitter sincerity*) May that day come soon! (*He pauses startledly, surprised himself—then with a sardonic grin*) Be God, I'm the only real convert to death Hickey made here. From the bottom of my coward's heart I mean that now!

Hickey has escaped reality by pleading insanity; Parritt by committing suicide; the derelicts by returning to their illusions. But for Larry, too truthful to lie and too cowardly to die, the abyss is constantly before his eyes. Out of compassion for the Judas, Parritt, he has told him to put an end to his miserable existence; and now he must bear responsibility for this and every act until his own life ends: "May that day come soon!" His desire for death is like that of Othello: "For, in my sense, 'tis happiness to die." The play ends in laughter, song, and the drunken babble of Hugo, as Larry stares straight ahead of him, a living corpse, swathed in the winding sheet of truth. Like O'Neill's, his tragic posturing has developed finally into a deeply experienced tragic sense of life.

This extraordinary play, then, is a chronicle of O'Neill's own spiritual metamorphosis from a messianic into an existential rebel, the shallow yea-saying salvationist of the earlier plays having been transformed into a penetrating analyst of human motive rejecting even the pose of disillusionment. O'Neill's "denial of any other experience of faith in my plays" has left him alone, at last, with existence itself; and he has looked at it with a courage which only the greatest tragic dramatists have been able to muster. *The Iceman Cometh,* despite its prosaic language, recreates that existential groan which is heard in Shakespeare's tragedies and in the third choral poem of Sophocles's *Oedipus at Colonus,* as O'Neill makes reality bearable through the metaphysical consolations of art. O'Neill has rejected Hickey's brand of salvation as a way to human happiness, but truth has, nevertheless, become the cornerstone of his drama, truth combined with the compassionate understanding of Larry Slade. Expunging everything false and literary from his work, O'Neill has finally reconciled himself to being the man he really is.

The Irrelevancy of Belief:
The Iceman and *The Lower Depths*

by Helen Muchnic

When in *The Odyssey* the companions of Odysseus are changed
by Circe into swine, they are not deprived of human consciousness;
but in Milton's reworking of the episode in *Comus* the men are transformed so thoroughly that they have lost all notion of what has happened to them, and are completely brutish and contented in their
pleasures. Milton, that is, in a way consistent with the severity of
Puritanism, changed the pathos of a state in which human beings
suffer from a sense of their depravity into the greater moral tragedy
of a condition so depraved as to make such suffering impossible.[1]
Eugene O'Neill's *The Iceman Cometh* and Maxim Gorky's *The
Lower Depths* are, it seems to me, a modern instance of much the same
contrast. But, although a comparison of these two plays seems clearly
indicated, the fullest one that I have seen so far is but a brief discussion
in the Russian journal *Zvezda*[2]; there, in the course of a long, and
generally scornful, article on current American literature, Vladimir
Rubin concludes that, "If Gorky's play asserts: 'Man—that has a proud
sound,' then O'Neill's *The Iceman Cometh* seems to be saying: 'Man
—that has a low and infamous sound,' for "the gloomy moral" of his
play "debases man infinitely . . . as a pitiful, will-less toy of fate."
It marks, he says, "the final 'spiritual capitulation' of this veteran of
American drama." This, of course, is the opinion one would expect
from Soviet criticism today; and there is, to be sure, a shade of truth
in it. By comparison with Gorky's view of man, O'Neill's is indeed a
pessimistic one. But this shadowy truth dismisses with too casual a
brutality the realms of concepts here involved. The whole matter is

---

"*The Irrelevancy of Belief:* The Iceman *and* The Lower Depths" [*Original title:*
"*Circe's Swine: Plays by Gorky and O'Neill*"], *by Helen Muchnic. From* Comparative
Literature, *III (Spring, 1951), 119-28. Copyright © by* Comparative Literature.
Reprinted by permission of the editor.

[1] This comparison was made some years ago by Marjorie Nicolson in one of her
lectures at Smith College.

[2] Aug. 1948, p. 200.

deeper and of a different order than that indicated by Mr. Rubin's remarks.

On the face of it, the plays are very much alike, not only in setting, plot, and structure, but in aesthetic conception; for they seem to be, and yet are not, "slices of life." They are, more accurately, parables of life; and the social outcasts who people Harry Hope's "cheap gin-mill of the five-cent whiskey, last-resort variety" and the "cellar, resembling a cave," owned by Kostilev, are not, despite the naturalism of their portraiture, pictures of real men, but symbolic figures in a parable on man's fate. As such they are exceptionally well chosen; the "dregs of society," as the mark of extreme failure, are distress signals which urge inquiry into the nature of human disaster and the responsibility for it. Both plays are plays of dialogue rather than action, and what is done in them, reversing the usual method of drama, is an illustration of what is said. In each, a group of individuals, loosely bound together by a familiarity which breeds tolerant indifference and boredom and with enough in common to represent mankind by and large, is confronted by a solitary outsider who considers himself, and is considered by the group to be superior—to this extent, at least, that he is in a position to preach and to exhort them to a new way of life. In both plays this solitary individual is the repository of a "truth" unknown to the others, and in both, after a brief show of impressive authority, he leaves the scene of his activities in the same, or somewhat worse, condition than he had found it. Is the joke, then, on him? Are the tables turned? Is the prophet false, or at any rate, inadequate? And are the benighted souls whom he had tried to save in possession of a reality which his supposedly superior wisdom has not touched? Who, then, is better, and who is right? Who is to be blamed for the melancholy outcome of events, the prophet or those who refuse to become his disciples? The plays strike deep, deeper than their spoken arguments concerning the nature of truth and the value of illusion. Implicit in them are comparisons between theories of life and actual living, between idealism and reality: demands exacted by the mind and those made by the body, hope imposed by the spirit and the limits to hope set by the circumscribed potentialities of man; questions about the nature and the power of the will; and a search for an ethics that might be accepted as both just and possible in a human situation which is seen to be desperate. But here, with the kind of questions posed and the way they are examined, the similarities end. The answers given are amazingly different, and as one studies them one becomes aware that even the questions are not so similar as at first supposed.

Each play is constructed around a central character, and its meaning hinges on the interpretation of this man and of what he preaches, for he comes with a well-defined faith to correct his fellows; it is to him that they are constrained to respond individually and as a group, it is on him that thoughts and emotions converge. He is, in short, a test of moral principles, and the spectator must decide to what degree he should respect and trust him. In their natures, the two characters are entirely different. Gorky's Luke is a wanderer who, not from any newly found faith but from an accumulated store of sanctified dogma, hands out good advice wherever he happens to be to whoever will listen to him. He clucks sympathetically over men's complaints, tells little moral tales by way of illustrating his precepts, and, when the wretches he has been "saving" are drawn into a perilous situation and he himself is in danger of being caught and questioned by the authorities, slips out unperceived; for, with all his show of self-effacing, greathearted sympathy, he is not unmindful of his own safety—and he happens to be traveling without a passport. Hickey, on the other hand, enters with a program of reform, determined to make his friends happy, now that he himself has found happiness; and until the end, when he becomes a self-convicted felon, he has been a respected member of society. Nor is his scheme a ready-made concoction of untested, pious maxims; his recipe is drastic, and he has first tried it on himself. In the case of Hickey, there is no question of hypocrisy, but there is in the case of Luke.

When *The Lower Depths* was first performed in 1902, Luke was presented as a saintly character, and the play was interpreted as a lesson in brotherly love. That had not been Gorky's intention, as he himself explained in interviews at the time and in an article of 1933 in which—having described four types of "consolers," the sincere (an extremely rare variety), the professional, the vain, and finally "the most dangerous, clever, well-informed, and eloquent" of them all, the coldhearted men who cared about nothing so much as their own peace and comfort and consoled only because they could not be bothered with complaints—he declared that Luke belonged in the last division. "In our days," he added, "the consoler can be presented on the stage only as a negative and comic figure."

Gorky had intended Satin to be the real hero, but muffed the effect by leaving him off stage in some of the crucial moments of the play. Satin is in every respect at opposite poles from Luke, whom he appraises with his native acumen and honest incivility. "Pulp for the toothless" he calls him, but admits that in theory, at least, the wanderer has the right idea about man: namely, that man is large and free and must not be hampered. Satin, who sneers when he is sober and is eloquent when drunk, who is not apart from but very much of the group, on the spot when he is needed, sensible, and, above all, realistic in his understanding of what his fellowmen can and cannot do, has an undemonstrative, genuine sympathy which is infinitely more valuable than Luke's facile, soft-hearted, self-protecting kindliness: "You know how to do better than pity," Kleshch says to him, "you know how not to insult." And his rhetorical speech about man, which begins, "What is man? It is not you, not I, not they . . . no! It is you, I, they, the old man, Napoleon, Mahommed . . . all in one! Do you understand? It is—immense . . . ," is the culminating point of the play and the one that states its meaning. From Satin's standpoint Luke's pampering consolations, when they are not positively harmful—as in the case of the Actor, for whose suicide Satin holds the old man responsible—are insulting to man.

In *The Iceman Cometh* Satin's counterpart is Larry, "the only occupant of the room," according to the stage directions, "who is not asleep" when the curtain goes up, and who indeed remains terribly wide awake throughout the play, who speaks "sardonically," with "a comical intensity," considers himself aloof from all human affairs, "in the grandstand of philosophical detachment," but cannot help responding to the sufferings of "the breed of swine called men" with a sensitiveness and passion he would gladly suppress. He is discriminating and stern in his judgments and penetrating in his grasp of motives. He is not given to long pronouncements, does not try to influence men, but his influence is felt in what he is and in what he makes people do when they compel him to direct them; and, when he talks, it is with the aptness, wit, and brevity of poetry: "their ships will come in, loaded to the gunwales with cancelled regrets and promises fulfilled and clean slates and new leases"; "when man's soul isn't a sow's ear, it will be time enough to dream of silk purses"; and it is he who finds the right name for the Iceman, when he calls him the Iceman of Death. At the beginning of the play he makes a little speech that could be taken as the theme song of both *The Iceman Cometh* and *The Lower Depths*:

> What's it matter if the truth is that their favoring breeze has the stink of nickel whiskey on its breath, and their sea is a growler of lager and ale, and their ships are long since looted and scuttled and sunk on the bottom? To hell with the truth! As the history of the world proves, the truth has no bearing on anything. It's irrelevant and immaterial, as the lawyers say. The lie of a pipe dream is what gives life to the whole misbegotten mad lot of us, drunk or sober.

The "pipe dream" is the obvious leitmotif of *The Iceman Cometh,* as it is also that of *The Lower Depths,* the real theme of which, according to a splendid analysis by the Soviet critic Iury Iuzovsky,[3] is the question "What is Truth?" The characters of Gorky's play, this writer points out, are divided into well-marked groups with respect

[3] Iury Iuzovsky, *Dramaturgia Gor'kovo,* Chast' I (Moscow-Leningrad, 1940), pp. 61-161.

to the kind of truth they believe in: those, like the Actor, Pepel, Natasha, and Nastya, for whom illusion is truth; those, on the contrary, who believe only in the "truth of facts," like Bubnov, Kleshch, and the Baron, all of whom delight in pricking, variously, the bubble of man's hope—Bubnov with quiet satisfaction, Kleshch with bitterness, the Baron with a kind of sensual delight, "sneering out of envy," as Luke says of him; and, lastly, Luke and Satin who belong to neither category, and whose position Iuzovsky explains by a reference to Lenin's article, "What Is To Be Done?"—written in the same year as Gorky's drama. "One must day-dream," says Lenin in this article, and, quoting the nineteenth-century nihilist critic, Pisarev:

> My day-dream may be of such a kind as to catch up with the natural course of events, or it may go off completely at a tangent to where the natural course of events can never arrive. In the first instance, the day-dream does no harm; it may even support and strengthen the energy of toiling mankind . . . In such day-dreams there is nothing that can prevent or paralyze the strength of workers . . . When there is a point of contact between the day-dream and life, then everything is going well . . .

comments that of the latter kind of day dream there is unfortunately too little in his time. *The Lower Depths,* says Iuzovsky, seems to give symbolic form to this distinction; Luke's is a day dream of slavery and leads to a dead end; Satin's is of freedom and opens a way out; the one goes off at a tangent, the other has contact with reality.

Nevertheless, whether they believe anything or not, the inhabitants of *The Lower Depths* retain, as individuals, a sense of their humanity and they suffer because of it; Circe has not deprived them of consciousness, and, even though they do not do very much, they retain the possibility of action. With the frequenters of Harry Hope's saloon the case is different. They are contented enough in their sodden stupor and are miserable only when, for a brief space, they are jerked into consciousness, for this robs their liquor of its potency to "paralyze." Once they are made to face themselves, the good-natured Americans, thrown into inward conflict by the sudden demonstration that their long-cherished beliefs about themselves are lies, become acrimonious and belligerent; the Russians, even the "romantic" ones, had been too sober and too unhappy from the start for any kind of pretense of mutual regard and general affability. In both plays, it would seem, amicable relations can exist only on the superficial basis of convenient indifference, the "live and let live" philosophy of those who have not chosen, but have been driven, to live together. The Russians have, indeed, much less sense of group solidarity than the Americans; all but wholly unaware of one another and much more callous, they appear to have theories about society but little capacity or desire for social living.

The real difference between the characters in the two plays, how-

ever, is not that of social relationships but of the kind of illusion they
cherish and the nature of the "truth" they are invited to adopt. If both
plays can be said to deal with illusion and reality, these terms have
different meanings for their authors. "Truth" or "reality" for Gorky
is not a metaphysical but a humanist concept; it involves not so much
a recognition of that which is or may be, immutably, as of that which
may or may not be done at a given moment. Freedom of will is here
based simply on a practical view of possibilities. O'Neill's position is
more sophisticated and complex; for him there is no distinction between useful and useless illusions, and no naive presentation of men
as fully expressed by their beliefs. From an objective point of view,
the "pipe dreams" here are all useless, but all are tragically inescapable and necessary to those who hold them; they are drawn not from
the human consciousness of Circe's victims, nor from their idealistic
hopes, but from painful, suppressed memories, the persistent iteration
of recurrent images in troubled dreams. Here every man has been involved in something he wants to forget. Circe has helped him to oblivion, and the one real victory of his life is his capacity to forget. These
men—all but one—unlike Gorky's, do not complain of the miserable
state they are in. Parritt, the notable exception, commits suicide. The
men of *The Lower Depths* are vaguely aware of some great solution
to existence which they have not yet discovered, and the play exhorts
them to seek a way that will lead them to discover it; those of *The
Iceman Cometh* have no thought of anything beyond their individual
well-being, which by now has been reduced to the form of drunken
senselessness, and the play turns out to be a study of the impossibility
of getting at the truth, indeed, a warning of the danger of going
after it.

It is in keeping with this condition that the "leaders" differ as they
do—that the American "prophet" is a salesman, peddling salvation
as he peddles wash boilers, required to persuade a sales-resisting audience of the usefulness of his product, while the Russian is a wan-
dering holy man, who preaches and consoles, leading despairing men
who are only too ready to believe him along the path of human kindness, soothing them with assurances that their dreams are attainable.
Both men are evil, Gorky's shrewdly and irresponsibly, O'Neill's, even
in his noxiously commonplace sentimentality, rather pathetically and
goodheartedly; for, whereas Luke's words are words only, Hickey is
disastrously involved in what he preaches. Comically enough, neither
accomplishes what he sets out to do—comically, because our sympa-
thies are not with them. If the tone of the plays is on the whole tragic,
the tragedy inheres not in the doom of the central characters but in
the pathos of various episodes, and even more in implications, in what
is not, rather than in what is, done or said. But if Luke and Hickey

fail as prophets, it is not because they have misunderstood the values by which their audiences live—a passion for faith on the one hand, a desire for individualistic self-assertion on the other. Nor is it these premises, but something else, that is proved false in their failure.

What is at issue in Gorky's play is the relative usefulness—and *usefulness* is here the same as ultimate good—of two ideals: one, the Christian ideal of tender, pitying humility and inactive faith, the other, the materialist doctrine of forceful, self-reliant, practical action. In O'Neill's play the issue is the nature rather than the practicability of ideals. Social activity is the sphere of Gorky's thought, self-knowledge of O'Neill's. Though both are concerned with happiness, in *The Lower Depths* happiness is looked on as derivative, dependent on an intellectual grasp of values: let a man become conscious of his dignity and capacity, let him adopt an ideal which is possible for man, and he will realize it as an individual. In *The Iceman Cometh* happiness is seen to be immediate and primary; larger concepts may be valid only as abstract formulations of what men have done: let a man believe only what he has achieved—otherwise he will be ridiculous, self-deceived, and dangerous. The reason Luke fails is that he is neither serious nor honest in his relations with men; but Hickey fails because, in his desire to arouse Circe's victims to their original status as human beings with insight into themselves, he has attempted the impossible, for most of them cannot be roused, and those who can will kill themselves once they have understood what they are. Gorky's "message" is seriously meant as a program of conduct; O'Neill's is a poetic statement of disaster, presented only for the contemplation of those who care to look below the surface of human activity.

Murder is central to both plays; but in *The Lower Depths* it is accidental, based on passion, and is generally conceded to be regrettable, while in *The Iceman Cometh* it is more or less premeditated, rationalized to appear as an act of love, and is not a mere episode but the essence of the play. In fact, *The Iceman Cometh,* the latest of O'Neill's inquiries into the paradoxes of existence, is a prophecy of doom, of the willful and calculated murder by man of what he thinks he loves, a revelation of his unconscious hatreds and desire for death. Always concerned with illusion, O'Neill has presented it in many ways: in pictures of individuals pathetically or tragically frustrated because of some initial mistake they make about themselves or that others make about them, as in "Bound East for Cardiff," "Before Breakfast," "The Rope," *Beyond the Horizon, The Straw,* and *Diff'rent*; in symbols not of individuals but of man overwhelmed by the force of unconscious primitivism latent in him, as in *The Emperor Jones* and *The Hairy Ape*; in parables concerning the ethics of Western civilization, as in *The Fountain, Marco Millions,* and *Lazarus Laughed*; or in psychological probings of man's soul, as in *Desire Under the Elms, The Great God Brown, Strange Interlude,* and *Mourning Becomes Electra.* Despite great variation in focus and interest, certain factors remain constant enough throughout the plays to make O'Neill's work appear as a continuous philosophic investigation of the riddle of falsehood at the core of life, in the process of which several partial solutions have been reached, but no definitive one as yet. His plays are eerie with the ghosts of terrible dissatisfactions and of desperate guilt; and their darkness is hardly relieved by a hovering conviction that there is power in love and that an ultimate beneficent grandeur exists beyond the groping and raging consciousness of man, for it is in tragedy itself that men are shown to have attained their desires. Jones, in death, preserves the magnificent isolation he had wanted; Yank, in the brotherhood of monkeys, "belongs" at last; Ephraim Cabot's desolate farm is still "jimdandy"; Lavinia Mannon, who has dedicated herself to the punishment of a wrong, shuts herself away from life as the final phase of her life work—and so on. In an ironic way, death and suffering are always the price of attainment, while back of this human scene is "an infinite, insane energy which creates and destroys without other purpose than to pass eternity in avoiding thought," and is sometimes called God. A primitive, necessary, unthinking, intangible essence that insures perpetuity is shown to exist in opposition to the will of man, who desires extinction. "We're always desiring death for ourselves or others," says Nina Leeds. "Our lives are merely strange dark interludes in the eternal display of God the Father!"

The Iceman Cometh, perhaps more clearly than any of the other O'Neill plays, is a morality play, a variation on the ancient motif of the Dance of Death, with its modern, paradoxical twist of willed chance and desired catastrophe, where each man kills the thing he loves because he feels guilty of his inability to love enough. Harry Hope's saloon is Everywhere, and the men in it are drowning a secret guilt they cannot understand. Gorky's outcasts, on the other hand, are boldly, openly immoral; they admit the crimes they have committed and are not ashamed of them, for their crimes, being offenses not against themselves but against something hateful outside themselves, have, in a way, the aspect of righteous vengeance. The depths to which they have sunk are only social depths; what troubles them is a sense not of guilt but of inadequacy, and to find truth is their only salvation. But O'Neill seems to be saying that to live at all man must live on a lie, for the reward of truth is death. Gorky's man can live only by facing himself, O'Neill's cannot live if he faces himself.

The theme of O'Neill's play is not really the difference between illusion and reality, but the difference between two realities: one the reality of belief, the other the reality of the unrecognized and unac-

knowledgeable forces of existence. Between illusion and reality a man
might choose, but O'Neill's two realities are not open to choice; they
are related to each other in a fashion so tortuous as to elude consciousness. A man feels and believes the very opposite of what he thinks he
feels and believes. And the reason for this is that the understandable
necessity to live has imposed on him a habit of unconscious lying; he
reiterates a faith in his will to live, in the great capacity and need of
love which animates his life, whereas actually his desire is to die and
the motivating force of his life is not love but hate. In short, the two
realities which inform man's existence are so profoundly contradictory
that consciousness must either pass them by, or deal with them in
falsehoods, or obliterate itself. Man is, by definition, a deluded being.
Thus the poor, harmless souls at Harry Hope's—good-natured, easy-
going, and rather appealing with their vague beliefs in love and honor
so long as they remain in their drunken stupor—exhibit, as soon as
they are forced to consciousness, unsuspected, deep-seated, murderous
hatreds. What Hickey's truth brings to light is that everything that
seems good covers up basic evil: Hope, whose life of inactivity is postu-
lated on the premise that he is mourning the death of Bessie whom he
loved, suddenly finds himself calling her "that nagging bitch"; Jimmy
Tomorrow, who thinks he has been drowning his sorrow at Marjorie's
defection, admits, to his own surprise, that he never wanted her; Parritt is forced to acknowledge not only that he is guilty of virtual matricide but that this murder was caused by his hatred of his mother; and,
as a piece of final irony, Hickey, in the very process of a touching dis-
quisition on his lasting and passionate love of Evelyn, inadvertently
blurts out: "You know what you can do with your pipe dream now,
you damned bitch!"

In Gorky's view, what men need more than anything is a belief by
which to steer their actions, but for O'Neill beliefs are irrelevant to
both morality and happiness. Man is born guilty—O'Neill's attempt
to rid himself of Puritanism seems to have brought him around to a
metaphysical confirmation of its basic tenets—and the more he tries to
clear himself of guilt the more entangled he becomes in it. For how
shall the kind of truth which consciousness reveals be met except by
death? What price life, O'Neill is asking, and is not genial enough to
congratulate man on escaping destruction by the skin of his teeth; for,
to his severe scrutiny of man, the death wish seems to have moral justification. The last of all illusions is that ideals are something other
than Janus-faced inventions, distressing and comforting by turn, without reference to anything beyond themselves other than the reality of
man's having to get through his life somehow. In earlier plays there
had been a gentler note. "Do not wound me with wisdom," said the
wise Kublai of *Marco Millions,* "Speak to my heart!" But now, how

shall the heart be spoken to when it has forgotten the only language by which it can be addressed, when all poetic vision has been lost, the great unanalyzable substratum of experience has been given over to dissection, love and hate have become indistinguishable, and the pursuit of happiness has ended not in enjoyment but in oblivion? More unhappy than O'Neill's men, Gorky's are not so lost.

The essential difference in the two situations is perhaps best embodied in the real heroes of the plays: Satin, ruthless in his appraisal of individual failings but with a native respect for humanity and an ardent faith in its grandeur, and Larry, whose cynical philosophy is coupled with an instinctive sympathy of which he is ashamed, and whose sense of justice is based on a hopeless understanding of human beings. With these characters, it seems to me, their authors are identified: Gorky with the man of action, closely involved in the fate of his fellows, but more clear-eyed, farseeing, and confident than they, and able, therefore, to inspire them by a persuasive vision of their strength; O'Neill with the Grandstand Foolosopher, whose function it is to look unsquintingly on man's depravity and, when called upon, to discharge the unwelcome task not of judging men but of letting them pass judgment on themselves. The high point of Satin's act is a stirring speech on man, of Larry's, his waiting by the window to hear the sound of Parritt throwing himself from the fire escape (for Larry's finest deed is to free a man of guilt by driving him to suicide) —just as the purpose of Gorky's life was to stir men to action, and the function of O'Neill's has been to make them aware of the full meaning of the evil that is in them.

This contrast, to my mind, cannot be fully explained by the fact that O'Neill has long been preoccupied with Roman Catholicism, into which he was born, while Gorky was always an agnostic; for these titles of belief may point to tendencies of thinking and perceiving but can neither describe nor account for an artist's original view of life. Some might say that O'Neill's sophisticated, puritanical condemnation of man has proved to be a wise commentary on Gorky's naive Homeric pity, history having shown that it is better for men to mope in harmless inactivity than to follow a leader whose promises fail to take account of the nature of human motives, and that Circe's brutes had better be changed back to men before being urged to action. But to say this would be to disregard both the complexity of historical events and the kinds of plays we are here considering: one of them has as its aim to state a temporary ethical problem affecting men in an unsatisfactory society which might be changed; the other, to scrutinize the eternal dilemma of how conscious man is related to unconscious nature—aims so divergent as to make these two samples of Western art in the twentieth century almost as dissimilar as those produced by the cultures of Byzantium and of ancient Greece.

Notes on the Editor and Contributors

JOHN HENRY RALEIGH, Professor of English at the University of California, is the author of *Matthew Arnold and American Culture* and *The Plays of Eugene O'Neill.*

DORIS ALEXANDER is the author of *The Tempering of Eugene O'Neill* (1962), the first part of a scholarly biography. It covers O'Neill's life up to 1920.

BROOKS ATKINSON, now retired, was for many years drama critic for *The New York Times.* He is the author of many books on the theatre. During World War II he was a foreign correspondent.

ERIC BENTLEY, Brander Matthews Professor of Dramatic Literature at Columbia, is a translator, editor, and author, best known for his *The Playwright as Thinker, In Search of Theatre,* and *The Life of the Drama.*

CROSWELL BOWEN, journalist and free-lance writer, is the author of the first full-length biography of O'Neill, *Curse of the Misbegotten.*

ROBERT BRUSTEIN, Dean of the Yale School of Drama, has been drama critic for the *New Republic* since 1959 and is the author of *The Theatre of Revolt.*

BARRETT H. CLARK (1890-1953), was a playwright, author, and editor, best known for his editions of *America's Best Plays.* His *Eugene O'Neill,* originally published in 1926, was the first book on the subject.

CYRUS DAY, Professor of English at the University of Delaware, has published *English Song Books, 1651-1702* and *Songs of John Dryden.*

DORIS FALK, Professor of English at Douglas College, Rutgers University, is the author of *Eugene O'Neill and the Tragic Tension.*

ARTHUR GELB is a magazine writer and has been associated in various capacities with *The New York Times* since 1944. His wife, Barbara, is a free-lance writer. Together they collaborated on *O'Neill,* the most comprehensive biography of the playwright yet written.

ROSAMOND GILDER was associated with *Theatre Arts Monthly* from 1924-1949. She has been involved with many national and international theatre endeavors and is the author of *Enter the Actress, John Gielgud's Hamlet,* and other books.

LAWRENCE LANGNER is an inventor and a man of the theatre, having been a playwright, an author, and the founder of the Theatre Guild. He tells his own story in *The Magic Curtain,* an autobiography.

MARY MCCARTHY, drama critic, social critic, literary critic, and novelist, was from 1937 to 1957 drama critic for the *Partisan Review. Sights and Spectacles* is a collection of her reviews. Miss McCarthy is best known for *The Group, The Man in the Brooks Brothers Suit,* and other novels and short stories.

HELEN MUCHNIC is Professor of Russian at Smith College and the author of *Dostoevsky's English Reputation* and *From Gorky to Pasternak.* She is a frequent contributor to the New York *Review of Books.*

GEORGE JEAN NATHAN (1882-1958), the celebrated drama critic, was co-editor and co-founder of the *American Mercury* with H. L. Mencken. A personal friend of O'Neill, he wrote about him as a man and a dramatist on many occasions. Nathan was the author of numerous books on a wide range of subjects.

KARL SCHRIFTGRIESSER was a feature writer for *The New York Times* in the 1940's.

JOHN S. WILSON was the drama critic for the now defunct newspaper *PM* in the 1940's.

SOPHUS WINTHER, Professor of English at the University of Washington, is a novelist and critic. He is the author of *Eugene O'Neill* (first edition 1934; revised and enlarged in 1961).

S. J. WOOLF was an artist-writer for *The New York Times* in the 1940's. The report of his interview with O'Neill was accompanied by a sketch of the subject.

Chronology of Important Dates

[Note: It is impossible to date the exact beginning of any of the great technological inventions that for the last century or more have been steadily transforming human life. But it is important to note that O'Neill was born in the age of the gaslight and the horsedrawn carriage, with the train being the only fast mode of transportation, and America isolated from the rest of the world. He lived to see, or hear of, atom bombs, rockets, and the "Cold War."]

	O'Neill	*Other Events*
1888	October 16: Born in New York City.	
1898		Spanish-American War.
1912	December 24: Entered a TB sanitarium where he decided to become a playwright (released, as arrested case, Spring, 1913).	Death of Strindberg [the playwright O'Neill most admired]; English translation of Strindberg's *Dance of Death*; a great deal of ferment, creativity, and high hopes for the arts in America.
1914	Spring: Composed *Bound East for Cardiff,* his first play to be produced.	Beginning of World War I.
1915		Founding of the Washington Square Players and the Provincetown Players, both noncommercial "little" theatre groups.
1916	Summer: *Bound East for Cardiff* produced by Provincetown Players.	
1918		End of World War I.
1919		The Washington Square Players become the Theatre Guild, producers of most of O'Neill's plays.

O'Neill	*Other Events*
1920 February 2: New York production of *Beyond the Horizon.* June: Awarded Pulitzer Prize for *Beyond the Horizon.*	
1922 May: Awarded Pulitzer Prize for *Anna Christie.*	
1928 February: Left for three years in Europe; the real beginning of his life of exile and isolation. May: Awarded Pulitzer Prize for *Strange Interlude.*	
1929 July 22: Married Carlotta Monterey (his third marriage).	The beginning of the Great Depression.
1936 November 12: Awarded Nobel Prize for Literature.	
1939 June 8-November 26: Wrote *The Iceman Cometh* at Tao House, Danville, California.	Beginning of World War II.
1945	July 16: Explosion of first atomic bomb; end of World War II.
1953 November 27: Died in Boston. December 2: Interred in Forest Hills Cemetery, Boston.	
1956 February: Stockholm production of *Long Day's Journey Into Night.* May: Second New York production of *The Iceman Cometh.* November: New York production of *Long Day's Journey Into Night.*	
1957 Fourth Pulitzer Prize for *Long Day's Journey Into Night.*	

Selected Bibliography

Andreach, Robert J. "O'Neill's Women in *The Iceman Cometh*," *Renascence*, XVIII (Winter 1966), 89-98. On how women make men unhappy in O'Neill's world, plus some observations on religious symbolism in *The Iceman*.

Brashear, William R. "The Wisdom of Silenus in O'Neill's *Iceman*," *American Literature*, XXXVI (May 1949), 180-88. The influence of the Nietzschean antithesis of Dionysus and Apollo on O'Neill.

Carpenter, Frederic I. *Eugene O'Neill*. New York: Twayne Publishers, 1964, pp. 153-58. How O'Neill achieved a unique blend of pessimism and optimism in *The Iceman*.

Chabrowe, Leonard. "Dionysus in *The Iceman Cometh*," *Modern Drama*, IV (February 1962), 377-88. The direct influence of Nietzsche's *The Birth of Tragedy* and *Thus Spake Zarathustra* on *Lazarus Laughed* and their indirect influence on *The Iceman*.

Dobrée, Bonamy. "Mr. O'Neill's Latest Play," *Sewanee Review*, Vol. 56 (January-March 1948), 118-26. A general appraisal of *The Iceman*, pointing out strengths and weaknesses.

Engel, Edwin A. *The Haunted Heroes of Eugene O'Neill*. Cambridge: Harvard University Press, 1953, pp. 281-96. On the role of dreams, drunkenness, and death in *The Iceman*.

Hopkins, Vivian C. "*The Iceman* Seen Through *The Lower Depths*," *College English*, II (November 1949), 81-87. A contrast of Gorky and O'Neill, to O'Neill's discredit.

Leech, Clifford. "Eugene O'Neill and His Plays," *Critical Quarterly*, III (Winter 1961), 339-53. On the terrors of self-recognition in *The Iceman*, with glances at Oedipus, Othello, and other archetypes.

Wright, Robert C. "O'Neill's Universalizing Technique in *The Iceman Cometh*," *Modern Drama*, VIII (May 1965), 1-11. How "identification with the spirit of man," the language of ritual, myth, and symbol, and "poetic density" universalize *The Iceman*.